# ALMOST FRENCH

Louis Jansen van Vuuren

# ALMOST FRENCH

*A life of fanfare and faux pas*

Jonathan Ball Publishers

Johannesburg • Cape Town • London

Originally published in South Africa in 2020 by
JONATHAN BALL PUBLISHERS
A division of Media24 (Pty) Ltd
PO Box 33977, Jeppestown, 2043

This edition published in 2021 by Jonathan Ball Publishers
An imprint of Icon Books Ltd,
Omnibus Business Centre, 39-41 North Road, London N7 9DP
Email: info@iconbooks.com
For details of all international distributors, visit iconbooks.com/trade

ISBN 978-1-77619-117-8
ebook ISBN 978-1-77619-049-2

*Every effort has been made to trace the copyright holders and to obtain their permission for
the use of copyright material. The publishers apologise for any errors or omissions and would
be grateful to be notified of any corrections that should be incorporated in future editions of
this book.*

Printed and bound in Great Britain
by Clays Ltd, Elcograf S.p.A.

# Contents

# Foreword

Mercifully for us, his thousands of fans, Louis Jansen van Vuuren – now in his early seventies – says that sitting back and putting his feet up is not an option.

Thousands indeed; for 20 years, Louis and his life partner, Hardy Olivier, have entertained scores of South Africans, French, Brits and guests from a bouquet of other nationalities in their famous Château de la Creuzette in the village of Boussac, in France's Limousin region.

In this book, Louis – artist, poet, writer, lecturer, shopkeeper, raconteur, charming host and friend – delves into memory to take the reader on a magical journey.

The co-author of *Festive France: Reflections and Recipes from the French Countryside* has, as an encore, penned these 21 stories that make the mouth water, the breath quicken, the laughing muscles flex and, sometimes, the hair stand on end.

At his very first exhibition, the teenager from Middelburg, a coal town in the former Transvaal, sketched a Paris that awaited him, a critic wrote. Louis made sure that his dream came true, however. In this dream, he becomes a figure who's larger than life in the French countryside, with one foot still in South Africa.

As a citizen of two countries, Louis uses brush, word and deed to shape the creative life that has made him the darling of so many. In this collection, his French odyssey is fulfilled, and he creates a world of joy and pleasure.

Salut, Louis!

TON VOSLOO

# 1

## A forest encounter

October 2019

The deer's eyes are amber marbles that glow like coals. When they blink, it's like something from a Disney film. The tableau before me looks just like a hand-painted stage set.

He turns his head towards us, his antlers like candelabra against the leaves. The stuff of concerts, this. Sublime. Any minute now I expect tumultuous applause as the curtain falls.

In my matric year at Middelburg High, we staged an operetta whose first act opened with the backdrop of a majestic forest scene. Every time the school hall's red velvet curtains parted, the thunderous applause from the audience caused chaos among the schoolchildren.

On opening night, Tannie Smit, who worked at AVBOB, apparently burst out crying and had to be taken outside to compose herself. 'I have seen paradise,' she sobbed.

Now, in the European autumn of 2019, I find myself at the edge of a forest in the French countryside, undone by an equally heavenly backdrop. I open the car window. The air is cool against my cheek. The turning leaves, the forest, the smell of mould and moss. It feels like I'm on a movie set. So in my best Fellini voice I yell, 'Cut!'

Hardy, my partner, cuts the engine and stares at the elegant animal that's now right in front of the car. The stag flares his shiny black nostrils as if he wants to breathe us in. My heart quicksteps through all four of its chambers.

From afar, muted church bells bring us back to earth. The spell is broken. I count four chimes, which means it's four in the afternoon. We'll have to move it to make the appointment with the estate agent on time.

When Hardy starts the engine, the golden stag pricks his ears, still looking right at us. Then, with a defiant flick of the tail, he vanishes between the trees.

We drive the forest road for another half a kilometre before stopping at the ramshackle house just outside the village of Lépaud. The estate agent's little two-tone car is parked under one of the cedar trees.

My pulse quickens. The quickstep becomes a full-blown military march.

The agent waits for us in the open double doorway. Afternoon light streams biblically through the stained-glass windows, creating a halo around his head and shoulders. Geometric Art Deco patterns in ochre, rust and smoky grey turn sunrays into spectacle. My first encounter with medieval illuminated manuscripts in Paris's Musée de Cluny comes instantly to mind.

The agent is a hipster with a beard Jo Black would envy. He wears a pair of pointed-toe Oxfords with no socks. Bare ankles – I mean, really!

'Bonjour and 'allo, nice to see you.'

Hardy answers him in fluent but businesslike French. The oddball, in his round, mirror-finish sunglasses, relaxes noticeably on hearing his mother tongue spoken so nicely.

He offers me his hand. There's a gold signet ring with a wolf's head on his pinkie. He smells of pricey aftershave and cigarette smoke. I look past his flashy sunglasses into the dusky heart of the house.

'Come eean, come eean.' His wolf-ring hand waves us into the large entrance hall.

What we happen upon inside takes my breath away. The spacious rooms have high wooden ceilings. Light streams in through the windows from all sides. The whole interior reminds me of Jan Vermeer's chiaroscuro paintings. It feels like I'm walking through one of his twilit rooms.

The dining room is an enormous hall with a floor-to-ceiling fireplace. The walls are panelled with hand-cut wood. The bay window, the full width of the room, draws the wooded parkland inside. You're constantly aware of the forest outside, which is visible from most of the windows.

Beside the fireplace, a set of doors opens onto a veranda. I can see that the scale of the place has surprised Hardy too. He shoots a glance at me as I walk out onto the veranda. It's a look I know well.

Whenever I get excited, outsiders often can't make head or tail of my meandering sentences. Everything I see, I describe in colours, in flavours.

My late grandmother Willemien would often warn, 'Cover Lewies with the *flenniedoek* to calm him down. It's the only way to keep this child and a rambling parrot quiet.' Then she'd wink in my direction, and spoon some extra *souskluitjies* into my bowl.

A stained-glass window at
our new home at Le Rembucher.

*Opposite:* The forest around the Le Rembucher estate,
outside the village of Lépaud.

Hardy lowers his voice. 'Stop with the senseless chatter. With every octave, the price goes up.'

He peers up the chimney of a stone fireplace. I feel a bit like I've been put in my place, and brush past Hardy and the agent. The wide oak staircase leads me past a second set of beautiful windows.

I stop and look down into the entrance hall. I start daydreaming about soft winter curtains on the double doors, an Aubusson tapestry against the wood panelling. I see paintings on the walls, the gold couch we bought in Egypt in the sitting room. Peonies in a white porcelain vase on Hardy's grand piano.

'The place needs *a lot* of work.' Hardy emphasises 'a lot' with a deep voice.

The agent rocks on his Oxfords, desperate for a foothold. 'But it 'as beaucoup de potential.' He waves through the air, as if he's wanting to do a ceremonial dance.

'I do *not* have the energy for another damn restoration project.' Hardy plays up the exhaustion in his voice.

I walk into one of the bedrooms and stand at the lovely bay window. The view is just superb – majestic trees reaching all the way to a row of willows on the green bank of a pond. I open the windows and hear ducks quacking. A cobalt-blue dragonfly whirs inside, flies a lap around me like a tiny helicopter, and darts back out the window. I look beyond the cracks and mould spots on the walls. 'This room, I'll paint blue.' Slender-bodied-dragonfly blue.

'Zees 'ous was zee old 'unting pavilion of the Château de Lépaud, who now 'as only une wall standing.'

The agent points to one end of the forest. If you look carefully between the trees, you can see a glimpse of the spire of the Château de Lépaud. He gulps the air and pushes the sunglasses up to the top of his head.

'Oree-gee-nally, ze château belonged to zee princes de Chambord, but was, 'ow do you say, ruiné à la Révolution. But zee 'unting pavilion was rebuilt in 1765, and zen remodelled in 1901.'

Another gulp. His eyes well up as if he's telling a sad story. 'And zen tastefully redecorated in ze Seventies.' He gestures towards a bathroom with a pale-yellow corner bath, rust-red tiles and salmon-coloured shag carpet that covers the entire floor. Hardy makes Al Debbo eyes. Not a good sign.

Hardy grabs my arm and leads me back over the black-and-white tiles in an overwrought tango. With a brisk 'We'll let you know, thank you,' he draws me with a firm hand past the agent and whizzes out the front door to the car, which is waiting in the shade of a cedar tree.

He reverses so fast that he drives straight into the stone border of the rose garden. 'Dammit!' He doesn't even get out to check whether the bodywork has been damaged. It's as if he can't get away quickly enough.

Hopeful, I wonder whether the accident is not, perhaps, the house's way of trying to keep us there. Filled with longing, I look over my shoulder and wave, resignedly, at the man on the stairs. His sunglasses glint for the last time in the late-afternoon sun.

We drive in silence though the forest. There is no sign of the deer. The light flickers through the trees onto the road. Where *is* the bloody animal? I wonder. I wish it would jump in front of the car and block the road, so we could get no further.

I'm beginning to give over to depression when out of nowhere

Hardy hits the brakes and turns off the engine on the gravel road. We're in almost the same place as we were when we saw the deer earlier that afternoon.

'What now?' I ask, wide-eyed.

He opens the car windows, both sides at the same time. The forest smells of ferns and moss and oak bark. His voice is thick with feeling. 'This is the only place on earth I want to live.'

## 2

# From Middelburg to the
# French countryside

My life is a colourful tapestry, woven with the threads of divine coincidence. Call it what you will: kismet and karma, fate and providence.

At 16, I held the first exhibition of my paintings in the Methodist Church hall in Middelburg, a country town in the former Transvaal. My daring and presumptuousness were richly rewarded when two reporters – one from *Die Vaderland* and another from the *Rand Daily Mail* – attended the display.

Both were very forthcoming about the talent of the knock-kneed youth with the cowlick. The latter had to have a dig at me because one of the paintings – the only abstract piece – was called *Midnight in Paris*. Had the youngster ever been to Paris? France, even?

Of course I had. In my dreams!

'Wishes do come true,' my mother said one day. She put her knitting down in her lap and looked at me with soft eyes as I sat drawing at the kitchen table. 'If you wish for the right things, and wish for them from the heart.'

I'd been restless all day; the wind was so strong that no one would dare go outside. The louder the August wind howled, the wilder and more extravagant my wishes became; my vivid fantasies kept lurching back to France. The laughter on my mother's lips kept willing me on to greater daring.

Not that I knew very much about France or Paris. But we'd just learnt about the French Impressionists from Oom Harry in history of art, which had poured fuel on the flames. 'One day, I'll show my work in Paris,' I said to my mother, my voice at breaking point.

Oom Harry – all the learners, even the principal, called him this – was the new art teacher at our school. He had replaced our beloved Miss Katinka, with whom we'd been in such good hands. I was very sceptical, initially, about this bald-headed stranger who'd taken over as our muse. But in time I started to understand this bohemian man whose zest for life spurred me on to let my thoughts take me where, instinctively, they wanted to go. Oom Harry, the madcap art teacher, taught me how to dream in technicolour.

In my university years at Stellenbosch, my best friend Philip majored in French. The classes encouraged students to learn the language's finer nuances through music. This is how I got to know Françoise Hardy and Frida Boccara. We bought seven-inch singles of Serge Gainsbourg and Jane Birkin, and an LP of Barbara singing 'L'Aigle noir' – still one of my favourite French chansons. It's believed that one million copies of the song sold within 12 hours!

Professor Fritz Stegman's film club met on Tuesday evenings in the engineering faculty. There, in the darkened hall, we'd stare open-mouthed at French movies with barely legible subtitles featuring legends such as Delphine Seyrig, Anouk Aimée and Catherine Deneuve. It was the Swinging Sixties, the years of Bardot and the legendary Jeanne Moreau.

The bunch of us wannabes saved weeks' worth of pocket money

for a rippled bottle of Dior's Eau Sauvage aftershave. In every advertisement for it, the iconic Alain Delon demonstrated exactly what a Frenchman should look like. We drove all the way from Stellenbosch to Stuttafords in Cape Town to buy it, because once you've traded Old Spice for Eau Sauvage, you're already half-French.

Where did this obsession with all things French come from? To the more sceptical souls out there, it could come across as an affectation, but I suspect it may have something to do with my Huguenot ancestry. It may be that a little French blood flows in my veins.

How else can I explain the intense identification I felt the first time I landed in Paris in the flesh? It's difficult to express. I may have had no command of the language, but it felt, to me, like a kind of homecoming. The convergence of the elegant people, the glow of the limestone buildings, the river and the art all around me made me feel as if I belonged there.

When I close my eyes, I can still evoke the taste of my first mouthful of *marrons glacés* (glazed chestnuts) – as if it were yesterday. I often think back to those early years in France. The only difference between then and now is that I've become more French in the meantime, and now enjoy this delicious snack with a glass of Sauternes or Muscat instead of with a hot cup of tea.

After my blissful student years, life cartwheels me around a little until – in 1998, eventually – I land in France, still in one piece, on the eve of my first exhibition in Paris's Rue de Seine. The gallery window proclaims the exhibition in full colour. I stand preening on the other side of the street, feasting my eyes on the posters with my name all over them.

Bursting with pride, I cast my eyes heavenwards to let my father know that he's entitled to boast a little about his quirky *laatlam*. When he bumps into the *Rand Daily Mail* reporter up there, he can tell her that it wasn't so arrogant of me, after all, to have given that painting at my first exhibition a French title. It had, in fact, been an omen.

On opening night the gallery is packed, thanks largely to my late friend and confidante Annette de Villiers. At 18, this former Bloemfonteiner was scouted to be a model for the Balmain fashion house, and is on a first-name basis with the who's who of Paris. There's a French film star or two, the musician Jean-Michel Jarre and his bright-eyed partner, and a whole troop of extravagant artisticos. My art sells well enough for the owner of the gallery to offer me a second exhibition right there and then.

I'm eternally grateful to the beautiful Annette for introducing me to Parisian high society. Through her, I meet the remarkable Hubert de Givenchy and the flamboyant Philippe Junot, Princess Caroline of Monaco's first husband.

After my second exhibition in 2000 in the Rue de Seine, Hardy and I make the unorthodox decision to look for a holiday house with a studio in France. The management of the gallery is of the opinion that, during the season, it would be a good idea for me to be closer to them and to my new French clients.

This is just the kind of talk I need to change my chaotic dreams into a full-blown obsession. Who am I to resist? There's also the matter of the sizeable number of francs in my wallet. And haven't I always been inspired by the thought of swaying gently in a hammock strung between two apple trees, a stone's throw from a studio, in a garden overlooking the Auvergne volcanoes?

Not long afterwards, Hardy and I are at a friend's house in the Allier region, in search of our own place in the French sun. After days of looking, we are despondent, ready to throw in the towel. My feet have never been so sore from walking.

The day before we fly back to Cape Town, Hardy and I make a last desperate pass through a few neighbouring villages. It is in Lapeyrouse that – at exactly the same moment – we catch sight of a piece of cardboard in the window of a little house in a crooked side street. In almost illegible longhand, it reads *à vendre* (for sale), with a telephone number.

The Hansel-and-Gretel house is charming, and fits neatly into our budget. What excites me the most about it is the outbuilding that I can turn into a studio with little effort. The narrow garden, spanning two plots, is an added bonus; I can have the vegetable garden I've always dreamt of.

Hardy takes his Nokia out of his jacket pocket and types in the number. And so begins our life in France.

A while later, we're sitting in a restaurant in Paris. The decorative window frames obscure the imposing towers of Notre Dame Cathedral. Further down the Seine, the reflection of a gilded dome shimmers on the water. I catch the distant aroma of chestnuts roasting over a drum fire outside.

'Exactly how far from Paris is your place?' our French friend Frédérique asks, taking a considered sip of champagne. Her manicured nails are painted a fashionable shade. 'Chanel,' she says, when she sees I'm looking at her fingertips. They look like wild strawberries against the bubbling gold in her glass.

'Three and a half hours south,' I answer.

Our tiny house in Lapeyrouse is practically in the middle of France: *la France profonde*, or 'deep France', as our friends call our new-found home. 'How could anyone civilised want to live there? Everyone is moving to Paris. The countryside is running dry.' They roll their eyes meaningfully at one another, then point at a magical shop window on the Place Vendôme.

The waitress takes Frédérique's order first: 'I'd like the confit de canard . . .' she says and, deep in thought, licks her glossy red lips before turning her attention back to us. 'Qui vivra verra (the future will tell). It's impossibly far from Paris. You're crazy.'

Crazy or not, our decision is made. It's a done deal – a fait accompli. We're investing in the French countryside.

The champagne cork arcs through the air with a dull crack, and lands with a plop in the fertile earth of my brand-new neighbour's *potager* (vegetable garden), a neatly marked-out piece of ground where evenly spaced leeks, carrots and cabbages grow. In the far corner, a few artichoke plants sprout hooked knobs of green and purple.

The whole vegetable patch is bordered by a double row of marigolds in full bloom. *Les roses d'Inde*, the French call them; I know them as *stinkafrikanerplantjies*. You plant the orange-and-yellow flowers specifically to keep pests away from your young vegetable plants. They are the gardener's best friend. It works, too. I tried it myself, and sure enough the pests stay away. Well, sort of. Maybe I just like the idea of Afrikaners being the keepers of the proverbial flock.

The cork now lies basking under an orange flower umbrella. Its origin is the green neck of a well-chilled bottle of Perrier-Jouët champagne. Rosé champagne. We've just verbally negotiated the contract of sale for our first little house in the French countryside. It's time to raise a glass, to say salut, chin-chin.

I know, I know, I know – a true gentleman and cognoscenti of good taste would never shoot a champagne cork like such a savage. In France I come to know that there's a specific way to open a bottle of champagne, and to propose a toast.

The toast you do like this: look the person you are toasting straight in the eye. Make sure that everyone has drank their toast before you take a sip. Never cross your glass with anyone else's, and don't put your glass down between the toast and the first sip.

I'm convinced that our French friends scrutinise us at every conceivable opportunity and rate our cork-and-bottle proficiency. French people are all born with this innate scoring system, hence their superchefs' obsession with Michelin stars. And don't even think about putting a foot wrong when carving a *poulet rôti* (roast chicken) or slicing a succulent *gigot* (leg of lamb). Non! Non! Non!

But back to the champagne bottle. First, carefully cut the foil just below the wire cage, then deftly remove it so that the whole of the cage is exposed. Then, untwist the wire, and remove the cage. Hold the bottle by its neck in your right hand, and push the cork gently with your right thumb. Now, turn the whole bottle with your left hand, until you've worked the cork delicately from the neck of the bottle.

A soft sigh should issue from the bottle, not unlike the sigh of a satisfied madame. A connoisseur never fires the cork; when this happens, far too much gas escapes from the bottle, which affects

This painting was part of my first art exhibition in Middelburg at age 16.

*Opposite page, above:* With a group of art students at Stellenbosch. I am on the left in the front, in the black trousers.

*Opposite, below:* At one of my exhibitions in Paris with (from left) a Parisian gallery owner, gallery director Laurent Deschamps and Marilyn Martin.

*Right:* A poster for my first exhibition in Paris.

*Below:* An artwork of mine in the window of the gallery where my first exhibition took place.

Louis Jansen Van Vuuren
28 Avril au 12 Mai 1998

the effervescence. In good company, low effervescence is far worse, and far more embarrassing, than a low you-know-what count.

At the end of 2019, by the way, France had exported over 1.9 million bottles of rosé champagne to the United States – not taking into account their own consumption, or exports to corners of the world like Gaborone and Helsinki! Not bad. Whether it's Krug, Cristal, Taittinger, Moët, Nicolas Feuillatte, the Widow or Dom Whatsisname, the pinks are way ahead in the style department. Rosé is the new black.

Our new life in the Auvergne, then, gets off to a festive start – our first foretaste of *la vie en rosé*.

Six of us sit, now, on the stone rim of a centuries-old well in the narrow back yard of our new home, each of us gazing out in a different direction.

Three of us are the sellers – two brothers and their melancholic sister, the grandchildren of the previous owner, their beloved late grandmother. The brothers are squat, short-legged and hairy. One is in a short-sleeved checked shirt and dark tie. His name is André; he works for the EDF gas supplier in a neighbouring town. When he moves, his trousers sound like static. Didier is the farmer of the two, clad in the standard blue overall of the French working class. A stumpy Gauloises Blondes hangs unlit from the corner of his mouth.

The sister has a good-natured face, but is given, periodically, to long, deep sighs, and her eyes cloud over, like a Cassandra of old, one who foresees things. 'A pleasant enough person,' my grandmother would sum her up shrewdly, 'but she takes everything so seriously...'

Then there's me and Hardy, trying to look as normal as possible, as if we buy a house abroad every day.

The sixth person is our friend Michael, who guides us with patience and goodwill through our first days in Lapeyrouse. It's he who shows us where the best croissants are baked, the freshest organic vegetables are sold and where we can get hardware supplies at a good price for the long renovation days that lie ahead. Michael is an art dealer who's had a house in the area for years, and who goes back to his home in Cape Town in Europe's colder months. I've often bumped into him at exhibitions there.

'Aahh, mais oui,' the gloomy sister sighs. In one swig, she drains her glass and drops from the rim of the well back into her shoes. For a moment she sinks a little into the soft ground, then smooths her summer dress against her body. Its fabric looks like a field of wildflowers.

They're all ready to leave, so we start the complicated air-kissing ritual. I'm not au fait with this way of greeting just yet, and often still bash chins and heads with new French acquaintances. When you do make contact by accident, and kiss someone smack on the cheek or lips, you're regarded with infinite disgust. Quelle horreur! For the French psyche, such intimacy is unthinkable. What I also cannot master is the phweet sound that has to accompany each air kiss. I struggle to keep my cool doing a simple waltz, so synchronising these movements takes all the concentration I have.

At last, it's just Hardy and me on the veranda step of our upright little house in the crooked street. In most South African country towns, the streets form neat, symmetrical blocks. Not this street – a diagonal exclamation mark reaching from the main street to the doors of the church. *La route oblique* – the crooked way.

We gaze, content, across the narrow back yard with its panorama of rich, ripe fields and green hills. On a clear day, the blue Auvergne volcanoes are distinct in the distance, a little piece of the blue mountains of the Boland. In our friend Ton's words, 'Now that's idyllic ...'

The essentials are all inside, waiting for our first night in the French countryside. Just in case, I've bought an enormous string of braided garlic. It's hanging near the front door to keep any evil spirits at bay.

'The place is haunted, Louis. The Auvergne. Even in broad daylight, I've heard!' a friend cautions.

All I know is that a magical song cycle, *Songs of the Auvergne*, has been written about this place. I once heard a beautiful soprano perform it. Thinking back to it now, I have to say that the melodies had a fevered, almost haunted feel.

But most important of all is the basket of food that friends have packed for us, for our first breaking of the bread in this strange village. A golden-brown baguette, a selection of cheeses and two good bottles of Bordeaux should keep the worst of the wolves from the door.

As I pick up the basket, I catch a last whiff of the melancholic sister's perfume, lingering in the glassed-in entrance hall. It's the unmistakable scent of lily of the valley – L'Air du Temps by Nina Ricci. Just like that and I'm a child again, seven or maybe nine, smelling my mother as she leans over to kiss me goodnight.

We're just pouring our second glass of Bordeaux when we hear a loud knock on the front door. Etched against the setting sun, we see the silhouette of the tiniest woman imaginable. The sun makes of her tight curls a halo of gold. There is an aged angel in our entrance hall. Her outstretched hands hold a steaming pie.

Madame Rochet, it emerges, is our good-natured neighbour and the village's most accomplished cook. What she proffers is a home-made *pâté aux pommes de terre*, or potato pie – a traditional dish of the region. This encounter marks the beginning of a wonderful friendship between the *fils de l'Afrique du Sud* (sons of South Africa) and their new French *grand-mère* (grandmother). I learn so much from Madame Rochet about rural French cuisine, including how important it is to eat and cook seasonally – and, like she and most of the villagers do, to plant by the phases of the moon.

Will I ever forget that first winter, and our floundering before the display case in the local deli? Inside it, all sorts of winter specialities were on show: ready-made dishes such as *civet d'oie* (goose casserole) and *flamiche aux poireaux en caqhuse* (leek tart with aged goat's cheese), and all sorts of terrines with strange names and even stranger ingredients.

I was so worried that the woman with the plastic cap over her bouffant was going to ask me something that I pre-empted her by pointing at some vaguely recognisable baked goods. Back home, we discovered – after a phone call with our neighbour – that our dinner, beautifully named 'pettitoes', was in fact stuffed pigs' feet!

Madame R, as we would come to call her, explained the difference between green and white asparagus. More importantly, she showed us all the different ways of preparing it like a French chef, for it to arrive steaming and perfect on the table.

Making our first acquaintance with a bunch of wild asparagus was also an experience. *Les asperges sauvages* have a delicate flavour, and are only available for a few weeks in February and early March. It's a delicacy that has been on the menu since Roman times. The oldest recipe book in the world – *Apicius*, dating back to the 1st century – contains a wild asparagus recipe.

But back to Madame R's steaming potato pie. We polish off the whole pie, *and* the second bottle of Bordeaux, and bravely climb the stairs to the bedrooms on the first floor. Enough Bordeaux dispels any fear of ghosts, and the garlic in the pie ensures that our first night in the Auvergne will pass unhaunted.

*La vie est belle.* Life is good.

# 3

## Rooi Jan deep in the merde

Lapeyrouse is a lovely little village on a beautiful lake. It has a Sleeping Beauty château, which definitely contributed to our dreams of a château of our own.

There are really only two streets in Lapeyrouse: the main street, which runs straight through the village, flanked by the *mairie* (town hall), the school, the *boulangerie* (bakery) and the bistro, and the crooked street that ends at the church, whose huge Christ-on-the-cross figure gazes out over the village.

When the church is lit up at night, the impressive shadow cast by this figure reaches over our front wall. Ecce Homo. It's as if, each night, the shadow guards us against the Auvergnat ghosts that our friend Renée warned us about. Against the band of itinerant Gypsies that everyone warned us about, too.

The pealing of the bells from the church tower on holy days is something to behold. During funerals, you'll hear the slow and stately march of the 'Miserere', with its sombre tones. Everyone in the village stops what they're doing and falls silent for a moment.

The stone-walled cemetery is opposite the bottom corner of our narrow garden, among a grove of wild apple trees. The funeral processions pass our little house on the road outside, drawing to a halt between the apple trees. The glass of the mausoleums often glints in the sun and I imagine, sometimes, that I can see the angel statues bowing their heads in reverence on hearing the opening chords of the 'Miserere'.

On one particular grey and gloomy winter's day, I paused, as I do, to listen to the bells and watch the funeral procession that had gathered in front of the church. The coffin lay in a shining black coach, drawn by two black horses. Each horse bore a plume of white feathers on its bowed head, and a black velvet cloak on its back. Their hooves on the wet tar road beat a slow march – a scene straight from a Charles Baudelaire poem.


We christen the house La Maison Bleue since blue has always been my colour. It's the colour of Hardy's eyes. Coincidentally, it's also the colour we paint the shutters – the first task of our renovation, so to speak, to make the house our own and put our stamp on it.

The second part of the renovation – or *bricolage* – process was a lot more complicated. The interior wall that separated the sitting room from the dining room just had to go. With my inexhaustible excitement – my gnawing impatience, rather – I manage to convince Hardy that a spacious, stylish room will rise like a phoenix from the rubble. A room we'll fill with chic French furniture, a testament to our decorating talent. In my mind's eye, I can already see the cover of the glossy magazine.

The ten-pound hammer is still brand new. Hardy takes it deftly in both hands. With a few well-placed blows, he reduces the entire wall to rubble. A cloud of dust billows around us. Red dust – the wall was made of small, red bricks.

When the dust has settled, it dawns on us that all the lights in the house are off and the fridge is dead quiet under its cover. What now?

Closer inspection reveals that Hardy's assault has demolished not only the wall but a web of electrical wiring too. It's a while before we emerge from the catatonic state brought on by this realisation. Hardy is littered with chips of concrete, wallpaper fragments, bits of brick and red dust. He stands, frozen, like Rooi Jan of old, the triumph quickly fading from his eyes.

Since I've apparently mastered a few extra French words and have emerged from the demolition relatively unscathed, it is I who must go down the main street to find help. The only sign of life comes from inside Madame Simonet's boulangerie.

Agnès Simonet is a tall, lean woman with red hair and arresting green eyes. She is always in a white overcoat and sabots, the French precursor to our popular Crocs. I have never seen her without her plastic gloves; she is ever at the ready to count out a dozen or so croissants into a paper bag, in no time at all. She'll then deftly roll the sides of the paper bag in to make sure the package is tightly closed.

She's ready to receive me, her gloves primed to peddle her baker's delicious wares. Somebody once told me that the French transform instantly when you confide in them, politely, that you have a terrible problem. If you lay your troubles as humbly as possible at their feet, their hearts will soften; they'll descend from their infinitely lofty heights to the base level of you as an *étranger* (foreigner).

'Madame,' I say, 'Madame, j'ai un problème très grave' (Madam, I have a serious problem). I repeat the sentence, dramatically, for maximum impact.

'Électricité,' I say gallantly, and gesture towards a dead light bulb in the display case filled with brightly coloured petits fours. 'Électricité. It went boom! Phaff, poof! Kaput! Finis! Klaar!'

When the old oompie who has come into the bakery in the meantime rings the bell, Agnès Simonet takes her eyes off me for a fraction of a second. She fixes her gaze back on to me very quickly, though, when I repeat my opening statement.

The oompie must realise that something strange is going on; without raising his hat to me or to the madame, he and his carved walking stick hobble determinedly out of the shop. Agnès Simonet blinks a few times as if she's staring straight into the blinding headlights of an oncoming car. Slowly, she prepares her mouth for the onerous task of communicating and says, with great ceremony, 'Le chef de police, c'est votre seule solution.'

The realisation of just how grave our situation is settles likes a black crow on my shoulder. If she reckons that the chief of police is our only recourse, we must be in big trouble. At that moment, all I can see is handcuffs and a passport full of red stamps shouting, 'INTERDIT!'

I go to fetch Hardy for moral support, so that he can come with me to beg the police chief's mercy. He still has the ten-pound hammer in his hands; what looks like the fallen Berlin Wall is still at his feet.

What we've done is completely illegal and childishly irresponsible. We still haven't been to the *notaire* (notary) to sign the contract legally transferring the house to us. We've contravened the building code and sabotaged the village's electricity. Surely, we are in deep in the merde.

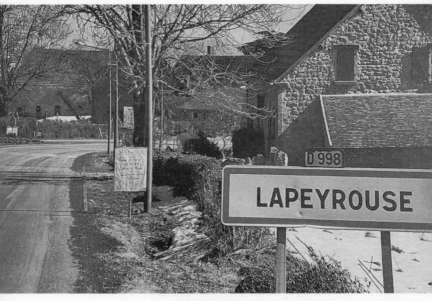

*Above:* The village
of Lapeyrouse
was our first home
in France.

*Right:* The well in
the back garden of
La Maison Bleue
in Lapeyrouse.

Lapeyrouse's church.

Our house, La Maison Bleue, as seen from the street.

My studio in the back yard of La Maison Bleue was
originally a bakery.

Our fate must certainly be expulsion from the Garden of Eden. Tails between our legs, we'll have to slink home, my mother's well-used *Kook en Geniet* under my arm and without us ever putting down our Huguenot roots.

In front of the police chief's brick house, a fierce black dog barks his ire at our foreign bodies.

'Let's just go,' I say, skittish. 'No one's home and that dog's driving me crazy.'

Hardy tries to soothe the black beast. 'Thula, boy, thula.' Good grief, I think. Whatever happened to friendly French poodles with silly pink ribbons in their hair?

A lace curtain with swans on it is yanked open a little way. It closes just as quickly. Before we can turn around to make our escape, the front door opens. An odd little fat man emerges from the house.

His ample paunch and dashing handlebar moustache are the first two things that strike me. Only the top two buttons of his shirt can close; the rest of his stomach is detained by a light-blue vest. His moustache immediately makes me think of Salvador Dali – and of Duchamp, who painted one on the Mona Lisa. The chef de police's moustache is one hell of an artwork. Black and curled into a real set of buffalo horns. He must spend hours every day – and litres of sculpting wax – on his toilette.

'Oui, j'écoute' (Yes, I'm listening), says Moustache, and silences his dog, which glares at us with neon-yellow eyes, ready to attack. The kind of dog that gives me the wrong kind of gooseflesh.

Mr Police Chief listens calmly to my Boom! Phaff! Poof! story. In support, Hardy adds a few easily identifiable sounds to my monologue, his eyes wide for effect, as only they can be – especially when he's proving a questionable point.

'You must have blown all your house fuses,' says the chief of chiefs in English with a strong Texan twang. Evidently, he had civil security training in America during the 1960s. This I learn later, on the authority of the omniscient Madame Robert, Lapeyrouse's resident gossip.

In the distance, I'm sure I hear the choir of angels, in stereo, 'onse Mimi' Coertse singing the highest note. Monsieur le Chef no longer looks quite so formidable or livid.

To make a long story short, Jean-Marie Delmas becomes our new best police-chief friend. He comes to the house to show Hardy how to fix all the melted wires from the blown fuses. He's presumably showing me, too, but in my head I'm already busy draping the nascent salon with silk curtains.


The locals affectionately call our little white Citroën C15 tjorrie, with its Dutch numberplate, a 'Sea Cans' – how the French pronounce 'C15'. South Africans would probably call the C15 a small bakkie, but it's actually a panel van. The smart alecs among them would call it a bread bin.

This little car would soon come to play the lead role in our, and our friends', restoration dramas. It would also become the star that ferries carloads of paintings to Paris, Monte Carlo and London, *sans arrêt* (without stopping).

Laurent and Eric, our kindly neighbours and our first real French friends, ask, once, what brought us to Lapeyrouse.

'We drove here,' I say, in French. 'In the Citron.'

They laugh themselves silly, and ask again. 'No, Louis – how?'

'In the Citron,' I say, getting irritated.

'Do you really mean to tell us you came to France in a lemon?!' Laurent teases, in perfectly good English.

The difference in pronunciation between 'Citron' and 'Citroën' (sitrue-hen) may be small, but the difference in meaning is much bigger. This is the first in a series of unpleasant experiences we owe to the delicate nuances of the beautiful French language. We don't know it at the time, but many more sour situations lie ahead.

Take, for example, the day I am describing our house in Cape Town to Madame R's stocky grandson, who is in the army. 'Là-bas nous habitons dans une cul sec,' I tell him, casually. I've heard the kids say 'cul sec', and am under the impression that it is a trendy abbreviation of 'cul-de-sac'.

'Sacre bleu' (Dammit), the young man says, the colour rising on his cheeks. 'You live in a dry backside?'

It's as if Afrikaans-speakers gargle their words from the back of their throats, while Frenchmen launch theirs lightly from the front of their mouths. Soft-mouthed, slack-lipped, they say the wittiest things, sotto voce.

'Faire la moue' (make a pout) is my French teacher's advice. It's the only way I'll get it right, is her courteous assurance as her red lips pout at me. For a day or so after those lessons, my cheeks would hurt; I'd often have to lie with a warm facecloth over my mouth so that my overworked facial muscles could recover.

Every day, I try to untangle my tongue from the grammatical predicament that strikes out of the blue when I have to explain anything in French that's longer than the two lines I've learnt by

41

heart and used to death. The exotic names of even the dullest of household items turn my mouth and cheeks into a deathtrap.

I start by mumbling the names of familiar things, over and over. It makes me feel like I'm walking into the lobby of Monte Carlo's Hotel de Paris with Catherine Deneuve on my arm: *fauteuil* for armchair, *nappe de table* for tablecloth, *rideaux* for curtains. It's in the bedroom, though, where my panic attack starts. I give you *housse de couette* for duvet cover, *table de chevet* for bedside table and – wait for it – *tête de lit* for headboard!

A double entendre is a word or phrase that is open to more than one interpretation, one of which is usually risqué. As if French grammar is not hard enough to master, the language is full of nuances in pronunciation and words with double meanings. I learn very quickly how easily what seems like a perfectly formed French word can burst like a shimmering soap bubble and leave you with egg on your face. You think you're saying one thing, but you're actually saying something else entirely. I begin a diligent search for the best word for 'Excuse me'!

Certain French words sound for all the world like the vilest Afrikaans swear words. It's a real challenge to swear outright with a friendly look on your face. Take, for example, something as simple as asking for a new camera or watch battery at the jeweller. 'Batterie' is the province of tractors and trucks alone. The French word for the smaller type of battery is 'pile', with a sharp 'i', as in the Afrikaans 'ie'. I still shudder every time I have to say the word.

One night, the young daughter of friends of ours started laughing hysterically at the table on hearing what she thought were well-known Afrikaans swear words among the melodious French sentences. Her father had to escort her outside. She didn't join us again that night; only later, when the house was in darkness, did she come back for her dessert. For days afterwards, she would start laughing uncontrollably without warning, then stop abruptly and stare seriously into the distance. The poor child wanted to study design in Paris; I heard she went to London instead.

Spring is sowing time, so early one morning I set off for Jardiland, a countrywide nursery chain. I'm looking for a fast-growing creeper to cover the ugly garage wall in Lapeyrouse. Laurent and Eric, who are keen gardeners, have given me the name of such a plant; last night, I practised for hours saying it.

When it's my turn to give the slightly squint shop assistant my order, I've rehearsed myself stupid.

'Bonjour,' I say, my armpits dampening with sweat. 'Je voudrais une pine vierge.'

For a moment her thick glasses fog up. I swear I see her trembling fingers feel for the panic button next to the cash register. When she regains her composure, she pushes a catalogue towards me and gestures that I must show her what I want.

After a protracted search, I put my finger on the picture of the creeper of my dreams. She gives a loud sigh of relief and blurts out, 'Ah . . . une vigne vierge!'

Those are the words I wanted to say, and really should have said: the French name for a Virginia creeper. In French, 'pine' is a terribly ugly slang word for a certain part of the male anatomy. Despite my strange request, I leave, eventually, with the right kind of creeper under my clammy arm.

It's a flaxen autumn day when Laurent, a real joker, compliments me on the shirt I'm wearing. It's light brown and woolly, with dark-brown and rust-coloured stripes. I want to tell him that it's old and well-worn.

'C'est en chien.' Phonetically, it sounds right, like the English 'ancient'.

'Quelle race?' he asks, surprised.

The French word for 'ancient' is pronounced 'aan-sie-ent' (the 't' is silent), but it came out as 'aan-shie-en', which means 'made from dog'! That's why Laurent wanted to know which dog breed's skin had been used to make it.

Time and again I see my arse, but the Froggies won't get me down. I'm also learning a lot about their customs, and am actually getting some things right. For example, the French often make a kind of slack-mouthed blowing sound. To make it, you keep your lips loose and blow out a couldn't-be-bothered 'pff' to show your nonchalance.

Note, however, that there is a big difference between an equine snort and the extremely refined French 'pff'. Also, make sure you never try it with a mouth full of food. I immediately start imitating it, regardless, perfecting the technique until I feel entirely French.

Note, too, that when you want to show your approval of something, breathe out as you say 'Oui'. Try it. Sometimes you exhale softly, and sometimes a little harder. It works like a dream, and sounds as French as it gets.

# 4

# Know your P's and Q's

After a few long weeks of hard work at La Maison Bleue, we eventually get our first chance to go away. We're dying to go south – to eat, to experience, to buy wine for the new wine cellar beneath my Lapeyrouse garden studio, whose antique iron wine racks, alas, still stand empty.

Hardy has come up with a fine itinerary; we'll be visiting fancy wine estates, eating in famous bistros and trying our first few Michelin-starred restaurants. It's all part of our settling in to France and, more specifically, our French culinary education.

We buy cases of wine from Bordeaux, Médoc, Saint-Estèphe, Pauillac, Saint-Émilion, Pomerol and Graves, and one or two bottles of Château Margaux and Château Lafite. We also buy a beautiful vessel of Armagnac in Eauze; in the south, we taste dessert wines – the Sauternes, the Monbazillac and, the most exceptional of all, the Muscat de Beaumes-de-Venise. This magical wine is believed to have been Empress Joséphine's favourite – she is said to have enjoyed a glass or two of its nectar with her evening meals. Her Napoleon was just as partial to his glass of sweet Vin de Constance, from the fairest Cape.

We eat bouillabaisse in Sète and Marseille, and are compelled to compare the two. We conclude that both are something to experience, but that the bouillabaisse Sètoise takes our prix royale. The cassoulet de Castelnaudary, the foie gras and confit de canard from Périgueux, the agneau de Pauillac, the green lentil dishes from Puy and the cargolade from Roussillon are also among our front-runners.

Our grand finale takes place at the restaurant belonging to one of France's well-known superchefs. Claude Darroze's celebrated restaurant in the village of Langon is part of a chic boutique hotel. The concept of the boutique hotel was still foreign to me at the time, but we decided we'd spend the night there after our last big dinner in any event.

After hours of sweaty driving around, getting lost, and getting lost again, it's late afternoon before we arrive at the hotel. It doesn't take me long, in the elegant lobby, to realise that this is a high-brow establishment.

The receptionist in her purple designer dress is posing and strutting as if there are hidden cameras all over the lobby. She barely registers these two tired and dishevelled étrangers; she points us to the darkest, most cramped room, right next to the lift shaft.

In spite of herself, she does make us a reservation at the restaurant, though. I decide that, at dinner, we'd better make up for looking so dilapidated when we arrived.

Hardy and I rush straight to the first clothing shop we see *pour hommes* (for men). He's dead set on finding something colourful. 'Black, Hardy, black,' I mumble. It's almost closing time, and the shop assistant has no desire to help us decipher French clothing sizes.

Back at the hotel, there's scarcely time to shower and shave before we're due to report to the restaurant in our new designer kit.

I'm dead tired from running around in search of the perfect boutique-hotel look. It's a look one cannot buy; only the cognoscenti know how to achieve it, and they're not telling. It seems to have something to do with keeping your shirtsleeves unbuttoned, even when you're wearing a jacket. And here I am, thinking it had everything to do with Tod's!

We realised back in our room already that Hardy's shirt was a size too small – and that my black trousers were a good few sizes too small. It was a real struggle to close my fly. I only got it right, eventually, by jumping up wildly into the air. I'm convinced that my voice is an octave higher for most of the evening because of the unnatural pressure on my diaphragm.

Am I imagining it, or does the lacquered receptionist cast a gentler look in our direction as her red nails wave us through the restaurant's huge revolving doors?

Let me just say right now that, like air kisses and waltzes, revolving doors can undo me altogether. Given my exhaustion and fragile disposition (not to mention my high voice), something had to happen.

The maitre d' is just behind the revolving door, at his lectern and reservations book, to welcome the guests and accompany them to their tables. He's a typical Frenchman: arrogant and a bit temperamental. His smooth hair has been gelled into the latest boutique-hotel style, his Gallic chin confidently high. A descendant of Asterix, ready for battle.

When I whip past him for the fifth or sixth time in the revolving doors, his smile vanishes and his eyes turn to ice. I wave every time I pass him, but I'm starting to feel increasingly stupid. I give over to the vortex.

When the doors finally eject me, I land right in front of him – so close that I can see the shards of ice in his irises and a few enlarged pores on the bridge of his aristocratic nose. By now I'm not only tired and stupefied, but the doors have spun me drunk. I take a few unsteady steps, a pirate on terra firma after a long sea voyage.

It's a watershed moment: I grapple desperately for the appropriate words. I've completely forgotten what I rehearsed earlier from my Le Robert & Collins dictionary back in the room. I mean to tell him in French that I've reserved a table for two, and that we're here, now, for the big occasion.

'Bonsoir, monsieur,' I say, and smile a little more valiantly before saying, with all the determination of a real De la Rey, 'Je voudrais bien manger toi' (I would very much like to eat you).

It's only when the full sentence is hanging between us like a windsock that I realise what I've lost. I'm defeated in this battle. And I'm certain the buttons on my trousers are starting to give.

The fellow looks intently at me, arches one manicured eyebrow and says, firmly, 'Peut-être après, monsieur' (Maybe later, sir).

Hardy has joined me in the meantime. I can see he's holding in both his laughter and his stomach to stop his shirt from ripping open. He can see there's not a trace of humour left in me, so he quickly asks for our table in English.

'Certainly sir! Just follow me,' the maitre d' says, like syrup.

I know, now, how Caesar felt in his final moments on the Senate steps. Defeated and betrayed. One of the points of this story is to show that many French people understand and speak English perfectly well, but only have the courage to do so before a humiliated and defeated étranger.

The whole song and dance of the starter, palate cleansers and sommelier passes me by without my registering much of it. I only start coming to when it's time to order the main course. I'm staring so aimlessly at the menu that the waiter is getting impatient with me. After his third loud cough, my eye falls upon one of the most expensive dishes.

'Civet de lapin,' I blurt. My voice is normal again; when I sat down, the buttons on my trousers tore entirely loose. The relief is monumental.

Hardy already has his main course when the wide-bordered plate is slid in front of me.

'Civet de lapin and blah, blah, blah,' the waiter announces.

I arrange and rearrange the dark-brown, stew-like slop on my plate, and take an occasional polite mouthful. It's not bad, but it's not great either. It has a strange taste and a profusion of tiny bones.

I don't even try to make sense of the mysterious dish. I pack the little bones in neat rows on the edge of the plate. After every bite, I reward myself with a greedy sip of whatever wine Hardy has ordered. The cheese and dessert also pass by in a haze. I don't know how we make it back to our room through those maelstrom doors and up in the lift.

It's only when I'm sitting quietly in bed with my dictionary on my lap that I can focus properly again. Civette. That's as far as I get. Just that one single word. Civette: a type of wild cat.

I feel the tears welling up in my eyes. Utterly slain, I switch off my bedside lamp and lie back onto the pillows, hoping that sleep will wash over me. France has won the first round and I can't get the image out of my mind of a goose losing a feather somewhere in the Cape. Maybe the morning will bring salvation?

And so it does. Hardy redeems me by explaining that I ordered civet, not civette: not a wild cat, but a wild rabbit. Made, indeed, in a delicious sauce of the animal's own blood. To this day, I still don't know whether the one is better than the other. But c'est la vie!

Salvation of another kind comes that morning in the form of a hand-shaped block of butter on the breakfast tray. It's Échiré, a delicate butter wrapped in a metallic gold serviette and packed in a *bourriche* (wooden basket). It has the perfect texture and a subtle nutty aroma. It's regarded as the world's best butter.

A slice of pain de campagne, a generous spread of Échiré butter and a tiny cup of flavoursome coffee make the morning seem filled with promise again. Like Ilsa in *Casablanca*, I say out loud, 'Play it once, Sam. Play "La Vie en rose".'

And immediately I add, 'Je ne regrette rien.'

Gradually, we learn how important it is to learn not only French but also French customs and etiquette. Look, I read Proust for fun (relax – the translation) and I know a fish fork when I see one. But here I learn that the French do things in their own fancy way.

When we first started, hesitantly, to go to formal French receptions, I wanted to run away so many times – it's that easy to cause offence.

'Non! Non! Non, mon chéri,' Françoise breathes from the corner of her beautifully painted mouth. 'You two sit first, and we follow your example,' she smiles, after rolling her dark eyes ceilingwards to the other guests.

It's our first dinner party with only French guests, and Hardy and I remain standing, politely, so that the guests can take their places at the formally set table. Gallantly, I try to pull out a chair for Françoise on my right, while Hardy does the same for Margot, on his right.

Hm-hm. Things are different here.

You give your partner a courteous nod, take your seat and smile at your French guests, who then solemnly take their designated seats. When the guests have unfolded their linen serviettes in their laps, you can get your party started.

Some French customs are hideous, very different from how we'd do things in Oranjezicht or Waterkloof. Others we find adorable. For example, when your French friends invite you for dinner at their homes, *never* take a bottle of wine or a bunch of flowers with you. Instead, have the flowers or the case of wine (yes, a case – wine here comes in boxes of three, six or twelve bottles, thank God) delivered to your host on the morning of the dinner.

This is truly chic. How many times haven't you had to run around, with six people to welcome on your doorstep, trying to fit another three or four bunches of flowers into your arms, and no more vases? This is just sloppy, according to the French. Send things in advance so that the host can arrange the flowers at her leisure, and display them with your neatly handwritten card in one of the reception rooms. Makes sense, yes?

Chocolate is the only gift you would dare take with you on the night. Be warned, though: the hostess will serve the box of chocolates you bring with the coffee, along with her own chocolate and any that the others guests may have brought. Forget about those Whispers from last Christmas.

If you feel you want to take a little chocolate something with you, do it with style. As the old French proverb says, money talks, but chocolate sings. And the very last tune you want to hear your mortified box of chocolates singing on your hostess's silver tray is Die Briels' 'Een aand op die trein na Pretoria'.

French etiquette is different from American or British etiquette. Here, it's not just about what you do, it's about how you do it. Le savoir-faire. Knowing how to know how.

Another lesson we had to learn was punctuality. As a good Calvinist, I always set my watch five minutes fast so that I'm on time – sort of.

It so happens that we are invited for dinner by the local notary and his chic Parisian wife in Lapeyrouse. At exactly two minutes to eight, we are at the door. I don't know about the flowers yet, so there I stand, with an armful of St Joseph's lilies. We knock and knock on the antique wooden door. After some time, Paulette, our hostess, opens the door, a faint frown between her lovely eyebrows. Paulette leads us cordially but firmly to the salon, asks us to sit, then quickly disappears back into the house. The lilies she leaves in my arms.

Lesson number one: in France, never arrive on time. Rather come 15 or 20 minutes late. Fifty minutes or an hour would be uncivilised.

Twelve champagne glasses are set out in the salon. After about 15 minutes, Paulette comes back, chatting and friendly. She takes the flowers to the kitchen. About five minutes later, a talkative Jean-Pierre, our host, joins us confidently.

The champagne remains unopened in the ice bucket. We sit, parched, for another half an hour, almost, until the last of the other eight guests arrive. Only then is the cork wiggled out of the bottle.

Lesson number two: if you're thirsty, have a drink at home before you leave.

Speaking of drinks, women should indulge in no more than one aperitif before the meal. Not two, not three. Jamais! (Never!) More than one, and you're labelled *une femme anglaise* – an Englishwoman.

There's redemption at the table, though. Well, sort of. Wine is often only served with the main course, very seldom, if ever, with the starter.

A few years later, when we turn the Château de la Creuzette into a guesthouse that South Africans would visit, it is difficult to convince the waiter to do 'le service sud-Africain' – the only way to get him to start pouring the wine the moment the guests sat down at the table.

Lesson number three: never, ever, pour your own wine. This is the task of the host, hostess or waiter. Even if you're dying of thirst. Rather drink your Evian – or, if you want to show off, your Chateldon. And remember: the big glass is for the water, and the smaller glass – alas! – is for the wine.

Put the slice of bread or the roll above your place setting on the table, and not on your plate, unless a bread plate has been set. This will also be placed top left of the forks, and not to the left of the plate. And, before I forget, salad leaves are folded and impaled on your fork – not, as is South African custom, cut into strips. Non!

Cheese is another story altogether. In most French homes and good restaurants, a knife and fork are set for the cheese selection. If you eat at people's homes, these are mostly already laid out. At restaurants, the waiter usually brings them to the table after the

For this table setting we brought a little bit of
South Africa to France.

*Opposite:* There is much etiquette when you entertain guests
formally in France, but fortunately we are fast learners!
We bought the crystal candle holders on one of our
many visits to the *brocante* (flea market).

main course. Choose what you want on the first pass of the cheese board; it's taboo for it to be passed around twice. (Having two portions of cheese tells the hostess that you enjoyed the cheese – the only part of the meal that she did not make herself – more than the dishes she *did* prepare, or that the main course was so meagre that you have to fill the last empty spot in your stomach with cheese.)

The cheese is eaten with a knife and fork. Start with the mildest cheese, and finish with the sharpest. Yes, you're being closely watched!

If you want a piece of bread with your cheese (never crackers), put your knife and fork down neatly, break a piece of bread off with your hands and eat it as it is. Never, ever, make a sandwich with it or use it as cutlery while eating the cheese selection!

Toothpicks can also be a minefield. A good guest carries his or her own in their handbag or jacket pocket, just like their lipstick or lighter. An accommodating hostess may leave some toothpicks in the guest toilet. In a good restaurant, or a French home, you will never see the toothpicks on the table with the salt, pepper and mustard. If you see this, know that you are in a tourist villa.

Please: never try to gouge that piece of salad or meat out from between your teeth at the table with your hand in front of your mouth. It's just not done. Nobody wants to look you in your watering eyes while you're scrabbling around between your crowns. Excuse yourself and go and do it somewhere private. Please.

If you do leave the table for your toothpick ritual, leave your beautiful antique linen serviette on the seat of your slightly drawn-back chair, and not on the table, where the other guests have to look at your wipe marks. If you push your chair back in all the way, it means you're not coming back to the table. This can cause consternation, especially if you don't speak French very well. Been there, done that!

French table manners, rules and traditions are generally a little different from the ones Tant Emsie and Nataniël taught us. But, as both of these trendsetters maintain, basic politeness is a good start.

France is a kingdom of courteousness. The words *bonjour* (good day), *merci* (thank you), *au revoir* (goodbye) and *s'il vous plaît* (please) are a good start. If someone says thank you to you, answer 'Je vous en prie' (you're welcome) or 'de rien' (think nothing of it).

At French dinners – as is the case in most places in the world, really – you're expected to 'sing for your supper': to engage and entertain the person to your left and to your right. Food, politics (yes, really) and art are the three main topics of conversation. But keep your money matters to yourself, please.

There's a lovely story about Coco Chanel, who once entertained a rich American in her Paris home because he wanted to market some of her designs in New York. The loudmouth started shifting around Chanel's beautiful arrangements of snow-white tulips, which she'd placed in a row of Lalique vases on the table. When he complained that he could not look the person on the other side of the table properly in the eye, she proclaimed from a dizzying height, 'Sir, do you not know that you were invited to talk to the person to your left and the person to your right? Launching your sentences clear across the table is downright crude.'

So, dear reader, when you can't catch the eye of Suzi in the hotpants, across the way from you, talk nonsense to your left and, if you have any words left, to your right. Your hostess has likely put her finest wedding gifts on display on the table. Sometimes, I arrange my table decorations deliberately, purely so that I can tell my guests this wonderful story when they start shifting my arrangements or candelabra around.

Over the past 21 years, we've learnt many of the French ways. But, when no one's looking, we've no qualms, on a Sunday night, about making Dagwood sandwiches with cheese and everything the fridge has to offer. We still have wine before the guests arrive, and we enjoy life as if there are no rules.

# 5

# The blue house and the stones of the Creuse

The little house in the crooked street in the Auvergne is our escape from it all for two exciting years. Hardy is still playing the banker in Cape Town, and I'm still teaching at the Michaelis School of Fine Art.

Over the years I've accumulated months of leave, and I spend every possible minute in la France profonde. I fill the flowerbeds with bearded irises and peonies, and revel at the sight of robins romping in the hawthorn bushes. I've only ever seen them on European Christmas cards.

I fill canvas after canvas with my new experiences. After my second exhibition in Paris in 2000, I decide to retire and move to the French countryside for good. For weeks at a time, sometimes, I'm left to my own devices. I relish this time to create, in the garden or the studio.

A friend of ours introduces me to Simone, who does small housekeeping jobs for people in the area. Her husband is in jail for hitting a policeman. It seems she works to earn a few extra francs, but I'm convinced she does so because she's bored at home and needs the odd diversion.

Simone is a beautiful, well-endowed blonde. More German than

French in ancestry, I reckon. The French describe such endowments particularly poetically: *Il y a du monde au balcon* – there are many people on the balcony. She likes her tight jeans and hot-pants, her bright, unbuttoned blouses. Her lips are forever red. She ties those unruly curls back, then lets rip with the Hoover.

I'm usually busy in the studio when she finishes up and comes to collect her wages for the day. The studio used to be a little bakery. It's wonderfully spacious; a few easels with half-finished canvases and drawing boards are always standing around expectantly.

When Simone knocks on the open door on this particular blue Monday, I am indeed in my studio, putting the finishing touches on a lovely still life with blue irises. Callas is singing at full blast over the speakers. I silence the diva.

'Quoi de neuf?' (What's new?) she asks.

Can't she see I'm working? 'I'm painting,' I say, brush in hand, faintly annoyed. I gesture towards her envelope on the table at the door, hoping the story ends there.

'Do you ever paint nudes?' she asks, pulling the blue ribbon loose from her hair. Her curls tumble in a mass of gold over her shoulders; she leans against the doorframe like one of those calendar girls who used to hang in the naughty mechanic Oom Ben's garage back in Middelburg.

'I never get the chance. There aren't any models here.' My voice sounds a fraction too high. I wasn't born with the caul for nothing: something's going on here. It's suddenly very hot in the studio.

Deftly, Simone's one takkie pushes the studio door closed. She unbuttons her blouse. There's sweat on my upper lip, prickling under my arms. I hear blood rushing in my ears.

Simone takes a seat on the high stool right in front of me. I smell her blonde shock's sweet shampoo. She loosens her bra. It falls, with her bright blouse, to the floor. I swear I can still hear Callas singing the 'Liebestod', or something equally Wagnerian.

I consider escaping through an open window, but a man has his pride.

Simone sees me looking at the window. 'Paint,' she says, looking me straight in the eye.

The empty canvas on the easel before me becomes my shield. It's on wheels, mercifully, and becomes a barricade between us. Just in case.

To bring her properly into view requires some acrobatic neck manoeuvres. I draw like I've never drawn before. When I've finished one sketch, I hurriedly clip another sheet of pastel paper onto the easel. The room is a sauna, but boy, am I *drawing*. My hands are crammed with pastels.

When Simone opens her mouth to speak, I clip another clean sheet of paper onto the easel.

'Don't move!' I command her from behind the drawing board. 'Sit dead still. I am making a masterpiece.' My hands are shaking like an old man's.

So it goes until the church bells strike six. Bewildered, Simone glances at her watch, scoops her blouse and bra up off the floor and hastily puts them on. She grabs the envelope and pulls the door open. My cooling system switches back on and everything settles back down in the studio.

'See you next week! You owe me overtime, okay?' she calls on her way out.

'Ne te stresse pas!' (Don't worry!) I squeal bravely from the corner of the room. 'Bye bye!'

I go and sit on the couch in the corner of the studio. Things could have gone very wrong here today. Talk about saved by the bell.

At a subsequent exhibition in Cape Town, the nine nudes are among the very first pieces to sell. I never saw Simone again. She and her husband apparently moved south when he was released from prison. I still have her blue ribbon in the little wooden chest in which I keep things that are dear to me.


Shortly after the Simone episode, Hardy decides he's had enough of tailored suits and silk ties and resigns from his job as a banker. Clearly he's heard the siren Gallic song – or maybe he thinks I need protection from aspirant models who insist on being painted?

La Maison Bleue is simply too small to be a permanent home for two. In every respect, we are both larger than life; the search for our dream house starts right there. Every time Hardy visits la France profonde from the Cape, we look at literally hundreds of houses.

We've become very fond of the Auvergne, broad-daylight haunting aside. The beautiful dormant volcanoes near Clermont-Ferrand, which you can see from the stoep outside the studio, have worked their way deep into our hearts. We nag the owners of the local château to sell it to us. Their answer is the same every time: 'Mais non!'

So we start knocking on the doors of every fair-sized townhouse, farmhouse and barn. We even go to have a look at the deserted school in a neighbouring village. I'm open to anything that has a door; I want to settle down as soon as possible, start living the French life in earnest.

Ever the sensible one, Hardy chants his cautious mantra over and over: 'Slow down, Louis, slow down. The right one will come up.'

There's the stone house with the shoulder-high, bafta-blue hydrangeas, the watermill we can convert to a cottage, the deserted barn in the middle of a cherry orchard. If it wasn't for the obnoxious power pylons along the border of this little farm, it could well have become our new home.

And there's the castle in the Loire Valley that's on the market. When the agent picks us up in a shiny limousine, it dawns on me that our pensions and piggy bank just aren't going to do it. We play along anyway, enjoying the pretence, the ten lounges, the twenty huge bedrooms. Not to mention the 45-hectare forest that surrounds the castle. I've always wanted to live in a forest. Wishes do come true, as my mother used to say . . .

We start scratching around a little further afield in la France profonde. The department of the Creuse in particular – part of the Limousin region – piques our interest. There are large forests around every corner; oak plantations have replaced scrapheaps and dumpsites. It's a clever idea of the French, to give nature a hand up in this way. There are now apparently more trees in France than there were during the Renaissance.

The Creuse also boasts natural water sources and the butter-yellow limestone that infuses the French architectural heritage. 'Les maçons de la Creuse', a beautiful folk song by Jean Petit, pays tribute to the special stones, and the stonecutters, of this region. It goes something like this, in my own words:

Behold the Panthéon and all the palaces,
behold the Tuileries and the Louvre,
the Odéon and the beautiful Notre Dame.
France can be very proud
of all these monuments
and for each one
it has the stonecutters of the Creuse to thank.

In days gone by, the stonemasons of the Creuse were true French heroes. This could be one of the countless reasons why my heart keeps returning to this place of blood, sweat and tears. During the 19th century, the first Sunday in March saw the start of an extraordinary journey as thousands of men and boys left their homes and families in the Creuse and began the 400-km walk to Paris to find work as stonemasons. It was early spring. There was much to be done on the farms and smallholdings, work that was left to the women and girls.

The men were taken up with a more important task, one of national importance: Paris was being rebuilt. Man and boy worked shoulder to shoulder for the glory of France. At the end of November, as winter set in, they returned to the Creuse. When the people of this region sing Petit's song with pride and conviction, there's hardly a dry eye within earshot.

This remarkable story is part of French history, from a time when migrant workers from all trades criss-crossed the country in search of work. Paris was the destination for which they all aimed, in hope. Every region was known for a specific trade: the lacemakers of Caen, the chambermaids of Bretagne, the locksmiths of Lyon, the singers of Haute-Marne, the chimneysweeps of Savoy, the coal sellers of Auvergne.

To return to the stonemasons of the Creuse: no one knows why thousands of stonemasons left the Limousin each year. There was ample space to make a simple, but sustainable living. Perhaps it was a matter of honour and pride?

The other reason why I'm drawn to this region is the history of its art. There are large lakes in the Creuse, and the dramatic confluence of the Creuse and Vienne rivers drew many of the Impressionists. Monet and Renoir came to paint this impressive scene. The region even had its own Impressionist movement, the Crozants.

The Creuse is a region that's full of surprises. The sprawling oak forests provide shade cover for deer and buck. French oak is world-renowned as the material from which wine casks are made.

The farmers fear the wild boar – or *sangliers*, as the French call the enormous bushpigs that are common here – that can lay waste to a crop in no time at all. The damage they do is so bad that the government offers farmers special compensation. The poor creature is also the most extensively hunted mammal in France, as its meat is in high demand. In winter, most restaurant menus offer civet de sanglier, stewed slowly in a rich red wine sauce.

The Creuse is full of beautiful villages and, legend has it, more than a thousand châteaux. If there's a copse of trees in the landscape, chances are there's a gorgeous homestead hiding in the green of oak and cedar.

One day, in an international real estate magazine, Hardy and I spot a colour photo of a weather-beaten little château in the middle of a meadow. It dates from the era of Napoleon III and calls itself

La Creuzette. We are instantly, hopelessly, in love with the grande dame. It's only much later that we learn that the flowers are incredibly persistent weeds.

Château de la Creuzette is smack in the middle of the village of Boussac in the Creuse. Boussac is an endearing village in a rural commune. An impressive castle towers over the scene. The village, with its stone houses that line the banks of the Petite Creuse, has been a farming community since Roman times, when it was known as Bociacum.

The popular French writer George Sand wrote some of her books in the 12th-century Boussac castle. During the 19th century, the castle was home to the *sous-préfet* (under-prefect, something like a local administrator) of the region. At that time, the well-known series of six tapestries, *La Dame à la licorne* (The Lady and the Unicorn), still hung inside the castle. The series of woven narratives enchanted Sand immediately; she wrote about their compelling beauty. When she came to the castle one day, however, the tapestries had disappeared. An elaborate search led to the realisation that the Rothschild family in Paris was plotting the takeover of these treasures. She wrote 40 urgent letters to Prosper Mérimée, the inspector-general of historical monuments (and himself a well-known writer). He was ecstatic when he viewed the pieces in the office of the mayor of Boussac. They had been rolled up; mice had already started nesting in their priceless folds.

Sand and her sidekicks convinced the government to buy and restore the artworks. Four years later, the *Dame à la licorne* tapestry series had been carefully repaired. I'd encountered the tapestry teinture (as a group of tapestries is known) for the first time as a starry-eyed, 20-year-old student in the Musée de Cluny, oblivious to the fact that one day I'd be living in the village where it once hung.

After seeing the photo of La Creuzette, Hardy and I cannot contain our excitement. The agent can only take us for a viewing in two weeks' time. It's impossible to wait that long. The magazine article gives no indication of which village the château is in, nor its address. It's only after driving ourselves stupid around a few dozen villages that we are driving down Boussac's main street, past a high stone wall. A stretch of parkland filled with trees sticks out over the top.

'There's La Creuzette!' Hardy shouts, nearly rolling the car when he climbs the kerb. The wall is high; it takes an acrobatic team effort to climb onto it. Out of breath, we sit like teenagers on top of the wall and survey the scene before us. The garden is in a state of neglect; it's been years since the grass has seen a lawnmower.

This palace is breathtaking. Surrounded by cedar and chestnut trees, it has a self-assured beauty; the shutters cling resolutely to single hinges.

'It's huge,' I sigh, discouraged, and start battling my way back down the wall. Hardy will agree, I'm sure, that the dilapidated old château is far too big for our dreams. He reaches for my hand and pulls me back up onto the wall.

'Wait,' he says, that look in his eyes again. 'We could always open a guesthouse ...'

aux armes de la famille. 300 m² rénovés : 3 réceptions, cuisin
douche, mezzanine, réception 70 m²; autre grange. Parc arboré

### REGION MONTLUÇONNAISE.
Village tous commerces. Superbe petit château sur 1,4 ha clos
de murs. 500 m² habitables, belles réceptions, salons, caves vou-
tées sur l'ensemble. Possibilité 10 chambres. Belles dépendan-
ces. Prévoir travaux intérieurs. Nombreuses possibilités. Cham-

An old postcard of La Creuzette.

*Opposite, above:* The advertisement we saw that
La Creuzette was for sale.

*Opposite, below:* Our first winter at the château.

# 6

## The keys to paradise

'Ce sont les clés du paradis' (These are the keys to paradise).

Duchess Marie Helene Angelique Sophie Eugenie Saint Gal de Seigner stands with her feet pressed neatly together in La Creuzette's entrance hall. Her black Christian Louboutin court shoes are spotless, despite the silver puddles that have gathered everywhere in the garden after a tepid, unexpected autumn shower. The water gleams, cheerless, on the antique blue floor tiles.

Her two-piece is the colour of the early-morning sky – grey, but not bleak, and unmistakably Chanel. Years of brushing and ironing may have worn the fabric slightly thin, but the cut remains crisp – a testament to the masterful tailoring of haute couture.

Just above her heart, a delicate brooch is pinned to her collarless jacket: a little gold sailboat with sails of gossamer-thin filigree. A female figure stands behind the mast, tall and proud. A beautiful dark-grey baroque pearl hangs from the point of the bow, clinking with her every move. I cannot take my eyes off the kinetic play; it looks just like the boat is under full sail, forging through a light-grey lambswool sea.

She holds a bag of keys out to us. The blue of her eyes looks misty and sad, her mouth more resigned than steady. She turns back into the house, leaving Hardy and I standing there, the bag of enormous iron keys – for opening and closing the gates, portals and doors of our very own little castle in this land of the French – in our hands.

We see La Creuzette from the inside for the first time when we visit the château by appointment early one morning. The avenue of wild chestnut, cedar and oak is so impressive that I feel like a child in a picture-book story. I can already see the hammocks and picnic blankets, count the drops of condensation slipping down the necks of wine bottles.

Inside the château, it is another story altogether. The duchess answers the door herself, and shows us, without ceremony, the salons and kitchen on the ground floor. Each room has high ceilings, with beautiful decorative cornices, crystal chandeliers and striking marble fireplaces.

The potential is vast, the odd crack or broken floorboard aside. One just has to overlook these. The walls of the dining room are full of stuffed deer heads. They look a lot like duikers, but are known as 'chevreuil' here. Their meat appears on every table in the village during hunting season. The overall impression is exciting, nonetheless.

On the first floor, there are five spacious bedrooms but only one bathroom, at the end of the passage. Each bedroom does have a water closet, though – a small washroom with a basin and a bidet. We will later have to replace 14 bidets with toilets. With so many bidets, I could make conceptual art, like Duchamp. Not that it would come close to his urinal.

Then there's the geyser that's been bolted rudely to the floorboards in the middle of the passage.

The rooms are all plastered with wallpaper from the 1960s. A travelling wallpaper salesman must have done the rounds in Boussac at the time; later, we see the same wallpaper in other houses in the village.

I'm no longer quite as gallant as I was, by this stage; when I see the second floor, my heart sinks. It also has five bedrooms, but the ceilings are much lower and the marble fireplaces are much smaller. These must have been the children's rooms, with a suite for the staff.

Words cannot describe the state of these rooms – suffice it to say that a tree had grown through a gap in the wall in one of them. Granted, not one whose growth rings you could count, but still.

No, I think, this is *not* going to work. Hardy also starts coughing nervously, a clear sign that he's getting uncomfortable.

The basement has the same layout, seven rooms with vaulted ceilings that are half underground and half above ground. There is something wrong with almost all of the windows; those that are lucky enough still to be hanging on their old hinges have no glass left in them.

We drive back to Lapeyrouse in silence, and go to bed without saying much. A short while later, Hardy's voice comes from the darkened room across the passage. 'Are you asleep?'

'No, I can't sleep either,' I answer.

Hardy's bedside lamp goes on and long shadows creep up the passage wall. 'What are you thinking about?' he asks, his voice clearer now.

'About La Creuzette,' I say.

'Me too.' His wrought-iron bed creaks as he gets up.

I flick my bedside lamp on. 'I've got a good idea. Let's go back and have another look. This time, we start on the top floor, where it's hopeless, and work our way down to where the sun shines all cheerfully through the windows.'

Which is exactly what we do. On the top floor, we reckon the château is out of the question; the condition of the rooms is just too bad. A creeper that looks just like a weeping willow shoot is growing through one of the ceilings.

Things start looking better on the ground floor. Hardy starts thinking hard and I mumble, 'Maybe . . . maybe this could work after all.'

When we come to a halt on the beautiful blue tiles of the entrance hall, we both yell, 'Where do we sign? We'll take it!'

The contract of sale is quickly drawn up. We even buy a few prized pieces of furniture from the duchess, which her seven children either don't want or can't accommodate. We do sell some of the antique sleigh beds later, though; there's not a South African in the world who could get any sleep in those short little beds. I spent a very long, diagonal night in one of them; that was the end of the sleigh beds.

Our good friends from the Cape buy La Maison Bleue from us, sight unseen. Hardy sends Anet Pienaar-Vosloo a few photos and tells her that we're looking for a bigger place. 'We'll take it!' comes her instant response from the Cape of Good Hope.

And so begins the great trek. The packing is ferocious. Where on earth did all these possessions come from in so short a time? It's all chairs and tables, pots and bric-a-brac from the brocante (flea market) – from an iron hammer with a decorative carved handle and wrought-iron bedsteads that have become sleeper couches to a stuffed wild waterbird sitting on a dry branch.

Allow me to pause, for a moment, at the brocantes, which are regarded as a national pastime in France. Every Sunday, during the summer months, villages host their own brocante or *vide-grenier* (garage sale). Everything under the sun is traded at brocantes, at giveaway prices sometimes – from pots and pans to mismatched dentures. Well-known dealers also offer their antiques there, however, and their collections of valuable paintings and sculptures. Sometimes there's even a cardboard box full of chicks, or a basket of rabbits. I once bought two fantail doves and a box of iris rhizomes from an old tannie.

Some brocantes have gained great renown, and people come from near and far to trade in silverware and rare objects. So you'll often easily find a Christofle teapot next to a headless Barbie doll, or an empty perfume bottle beside a Daum crystal vase. You're expected to haggle, within reason, and there are broad smiles all around for each bargain that people find.

A brocante is a big affair; there's usually an ox or a pig turning smokily on a spit, soft-serve ice cream melting stickily all over your hands, and the universal *barbe à papa* (candy floss on a stick). Music plays, and everyone is happy. The rosé and *bières blondes* (lagers) are drunk with gusto.

What makes the brocantes so exciting for the thousands of vultures who descend on the villages in the summer is the chance of your discovering a Monet or a Picasso. Really! Not long ago, an excited Pole bought a badly damaged Van Gogh in a village near Arles, in the south of France. The still life with quinces and nasturtiums had been used to reinforce the gate of a chicken coop on a farm. When this find was publicised, a television crew descended on the poor farmer and his wife. They turned the farm upside down in search of a second potential masterpiece. But alas, there were only a few old clogs up in the attic. When they asked the farmer's wife whether she regretted selling the treasured artwork, she answered, 'Phoooey, I don't even like quinces and with the €50 I could fix the gate of the chicken coop really nicely. To tell the truth, I could buy a whole roll of netting with it.' She laughed, and her gums flashed pink.

A brocante can be as small as a few tables around the town hall – or it can take over an entire village. The famous Braderie de Lille boasts over 200 km of exhibition space, with several parking areas for the thousands of visitors. Some of the big brocantes in the south have got so out of hand that the salesladies stand around in their heels with lists giving the dollar price of the most sought-after items.

We manage to pack everything we own, eventually. We drive the C15 silly between Lapeyrouse and Boussac, and wait with great excitement for the exodus from Africa. The things we value most are shipped to Marseille, and trucked to La Creuzette's doorstep. And so, at last, we start unpacking, on a grey January day at La Creuzette.


La Creuzette has always been a house for summer holidays, so it has no central heating. Evidently, the duchess and her family installed themselves in front of the many fireplaces on chilly nights.

On our way to La Creuzette
with a new fridge on the roof of the C15.

Fooling around in the snow.

Since we'll be living here year-round, we need to think about heating, but we're not in any hurry to make this pricey decision. I've always thought that the French make a mountain out of a molehill when it comes to the cold, and that my string of electric DeLonghi heaters would keep us cosy and snug. Which they do, for the first three sunny days of our occupation. Granted, I did need to double up on thermal underwear, but *tout va bien* (everything is fine).

But then, one dark night, the mercury dips to −15 °C. I shiver myself awake at just after four in the morning. Initially, I think Hardy must have tuned in to a Spanish radio station to cheer me up – but what I'm hearing is the chattering of my ceramic crowns. There's no time to waste. I leap out of bed and plug in a third De-Longhi and turn it right up to maximum heat.

Phafff!

Sparks fly through the dawn gloom; the smell of charred electrical wire hangs in a dirty blue cloud above my little herd of doused heaters. The lights still work, but all the wall plugs are out of action.

Needs must; I wriggle my last set of thermal underwear over my sleepshirt and add my leather jacket, hiking socks, ugly purple woollen scarf and yes, finally, a Kangol beanie, which I pull all the way down to my eyebrows. Buried under a wagonload of blankets and my great-grandmother's rabbit-fur kaross, my thoughts lead to Racheltjie de Beer and I lapse into an icy swoon.

It is easily three days before Hardy and a friend, whom we call Lynn die Boerin (Lynn the 'Farmeress'), try to lure me out of my down-and-pelt shelter. I unwrap the tiniest bit of snout and greet them distractedly. Lynn's voice is full of compassion: 'Look, Loeiste (as she calls me), I've brought you a saviour.'

My snout pushes a little further out of the bedding. A tall, thin man stands in the doorway. He makes me think instantly of my collection of old movie posters: he looks just like Clint Eastwood in *The Good, the Bad and the Ugly*.

My saviour is Bernard Bollinger (no relation, sadly, to the champagne family), an electrician in a pair of red cowboy boots. He's wiring an emergency cable from the basement to my bedroom so that I can switch my beloved DeLonghis back on and start to thaw. He drills holes like a real strongman through the thick stone walls; before long, he lays a thick black electrical wire down just next to my bed. I can plug my heater herd back in without causing complete devastation.

A day or so later I'm defrosted, and can dare to get up wearing only two layers of everything. I have to say that the aromas from the kitchen, where a generous *pot-au-feu* (potjiekos) is bubbling, contribute greatly to my newly acquired mobility.

The meeting with the heating company's saleswoman happens right there in my bedroom. Needless to say, it's been some time since price was the primary consideration. She leaves in her shiny leather heels with the promise that they'll start the installation after the weekend if we approve the quote.

I promise her with all my heart that she can cue up her team for the coming Monday. February, the coldest month in France, lies ahead. I plan to be ready when its frosty, grey skirt settles on the horizon.

The wise ones say you never own a château – that the château owns you. Something to contemplate when, just weeks later, I'm turning the dial on the heating panel up just a little further, pulling the cork out of a Châteauneuf and watching, in great comfort, the first snowflakes fall.

# 7

# Concrete is the new bronze

'Dear sir, last night, not far from here, my beloved wife's nephew was kicked to death in a muddy field by a carthorse. I come, with my grieving family, to your village market to scrape together a few miserable euros through the kindness of strangers – for a decent coffin and a humble burial.'

The words slip uninterrupted from the Gypsy's mouth, over his chapped lips. There's a deep cleft in his chin, like the actor Kirk Douglas's.

'I can see, dear sir, that you're the kind of person who can feel the pain of another in his heart.'

His clammy hand gives my arm a few impassioned squeezes ... is that a tear I see in his eye? The scent of cheap tobacco and garlic steams warm against my clean-shaven cheek. There's a brown tobacco wad in the corner of his mouth.

With blinding speed, the dull-green five-euro note is folded double and slipped deep into his pocket. I quickly turn away and disappear between the vegetable stalls.

'May the gods bless you, sir!' he calls behind me.

His words follow me to a table full of spanspek, where I seek shelter. Out of pure confusion I want to pick one up, smell it and squeeze it, but by now I know better. If you ever want to see all hell break loose, touch or pick up French fruits or vegetables. Jamais! On one spring morning, at the very beginning of our life in Boussac, in pure amazement I picked up and smelled a branch of vine tomatoes. It was heavenly, the velvety-green branch with its 15 perfect robin-red tomatoes. Did the farm tannie ever shatter my reverie; I had to use the front of my shirt to wipe the spittle from my new sunglasses. To this day, I walk a detour around her stall.

There are over three million Gypsies, or Roma, in France, many of them in and around villages in the countryside. They spend their whole lives travelling from village to village within the same department. Etymologically speaking, the word 'Gypsy' comes from the Greek 'atsingani' which, in the 9th century, referred to an itinerant group of people who liked to make music and do magic tricks; unfortunately, they developed a reputation for stealing. The French use the words 'gitan', 'tzigane', 'bohémiens' and 'gens du voyage' (nomads) to refer to them.

It's common knowledge that the Roma (a name that has nothing to do with the city of Rome) originated from the Punjab and Rajasthan regions of India, and that they migrated via the Iranian escarpment to Europe – landing, ultimately, in France via Bohemia. Hence the reference to 'bohémiens'.

What many people don't know – or don't want to know – is that this colourful group of people have been cruelly mistreated. During the Nazi regime, over a million Gypsies were murdered, many of them exterminated in labour camps. Until the late 1970s, it was law in Norway and what is now the Czech Republic that Gypsy women had to be sterilised after their first child.

Today, Unesco and other United Nations agencies are making

a concerted effort to improve the circumstances of Gypsy groups. The hand-painted caravans they used to live in are making way for panel vans, predominantly white Mercedes-Benzes, which often sport a satellite dish on the roof. No one wants to miss World Cup soccer or *Grey's Anatomy*.

Sometimes you'll drive past a long, white cavalcade, or see the camps they make at the edges of town, bright washing flapping between the panel vans. There is always a *brak* or three scratching around between the rubbish and the drum fires for a chop bone.

Or you'll notice them suddenly, one day, at your local village market. Often, the women sell simple bunches of wildflowers, a jug of bone-white arum lilies, a delicate bunch of purple violets. Some of the women march straight up to you; before you know it, one will have taken your hand in hers and started reading your palm as if she's looking for the highway to Paris.

The men stand around, their hands thrust deep into the pockets of their shiny black trousers, searching for eyes to make contact with – to open the way for talking you into buying something or accepting a service they offer you. They can fix chairs and replace the weathered tin linings of sought-after French copper pots and pans.

One night, we drive into a Gypsy camp near Boussac. The white panel vans are parked around a rustic house, and a huge fire burns high in the centre of the yard. The group has gathered in a circle around the fire. Curious, I switch off the engine and open the window. Two men rock and sway, playing the most riveting violin music. Instruments clasped firmly under their chins, they sweep their bows through the night air. Like the night, the music is filled with fire, a palpable nostalgia, a deep yearning for something lost.

A young Gypsy girl rises, in the circle, and starts to sing a song that makes the hair stand up all the way down my spine. I don't understand a word she is singing, but the melody, steeped with emotion, is distantly familiar. Her face keeps changing in the red-and-orange glow of the fire.

Maybe there's a splash of Gypsy in us all. I knew, that night, that I too could pack a caravan and make the never-ending, winding road my home. We drive home in quietude; I gaze once more at the Milky Way through my open window before I draw the curtains.

The next morning, I still feel that sense of otherness – until, that is, I hear Hardy curse at the top of his voice in the garden. All four of our hubcaps, and the C15's rear numberplate, are gone; I turn off the CD of Liszt's Gypsy dances and tune the radio to Nostalgie.


This is not, unfortunately, the last time we're exposed to Gypsy habits. The other occasion is a festival weekend in Boussac. The village is bustling, the main square's pavement cafés packed with visitors and locals. The stalls are crammed with *kaggelkak*, home bakes, glazed fruit and barbe à papa. Music and voices sputter over the cobblestones. The flickering of the lights is enchanting, casting shadows on the horses of the ever-wheeling carousel, their glazed and searching eyes, the restless children.

Preoccupied, a youngish Gypsy man in a floppy velvet cap turns the crank of his barrel organ. A melancholic melody from the south – 'La Java Bleue'. A little wire-haired dog lies meekly on a threadbare yellow baby blanket, listening to the sweet sounds of his master's mournful song. An Orangina can, cut open, waits for change.

The carousing lasts all night; earplugs notwithstanding, I wake tired and stale. On our way to the bakery for our daily croissants, I discover, to my shock, that our life-sized Diana, goddess of the hunt, has vanished from her plinth in the night.

I see, too, that Hermes, messenger of the gods, who lived on the other side of the tree-lined avenue, is also gone. We bought Diana and Hermes when we were still in Cape Town, from a friendly Italian woman, and brought them to Boussac with our garden furniture and a few other things.

The tracks in the dewy grass testify clearly that a harness of some kind was used to kidnap our concrete gods in the night. The hole cut neatly in the fence, which replaced a small section of wall damaged after a tree collapsed onto it, is the final proof of what happened in the night in the garden of La Creuzette.

When the two statues arrived in France, I placed them prominently in the front garden but soon realised that they looked far too dull and white against the dark green of the trees. So, I got stuck into them with paint and brush, transforming the concrete figures into bronze gods. Once I'd polished them with beeswax, they stood out beautifully against the green of the parkland.

In the meantime, our friends Anet and Ton Vosloo had become our neighbours. They bought the house next door before it had even gone on the market, so eager were they to live *la vie française* with us. A big restoration project was on the go next door; we put a gate in the wall between our houses so that we could come and go unobstructed.

Hardy and Anet Pienaar-Vosloo after a shopping
expedition for lights.

Ton Vosloo and I
make clafoutis.

*Opposite:* Hardy
on the scaffold in
La Creuzette's
kitchen.

Anet comes over to see the two empty spots on the lawn, and we go to the police station together. Without even a mouthful of croissant.

I must have rang the bell 20 times before Brigadier (Sergeant) Du Pont greets us in her husky Gauloises voice. She can't seem to hear me very well this morning; I repeat my story a few times into the grey microphone of the intercom system. In France, you need to make an appointment to speak to a police officer. You don't just barge in like a whirlwind!

She must have given up on the intercom: while I'm busy telling the little metal box my story for the umpteenth time, she suddenly appears before us. It takes us about an hour and a half to fill in the 30 required forms. Du Pont writes with her left hand, if you could call it writing. There's a dark rust-coloured nicotine stain between her index finger and middle finger.

Anet has to rush home to her photo albums and cut them up so that we can submit photos of the two statues. How can the police launch a search if they don't know what the objects in question look like?, Du Pont asks, frowning.

Two weeks later, I'm just about to put a nice chunk of baguette, with a thick slice of Brie and dripping fig preserve on it, into my greedy mouth, when the phone rings. It's Brigadier Du Pont, who informs me triumphantly that I need to contact the police in Gouzon, south of Boussac, in connection with certain stolen goods. No, she cannot furnish me with the telephone number. I must look it up in the local directory myself.

Our tjorrie is in the workshop for acute exhaustion. Luckily, Anet has a fleet-footed navy-blue Peugeot station wagon. We're there in a flash, only to hear that we need to fill in another 40 forms. In three different colours, this time: yellow, white and green.

That done, a bearded young policeman leads us to the storage rooms off the square outside. There they are, our fallen gods. Both Diana and Hermes are headless; Hermes came off worst, with not only two missing arms but a fractured foot too. With difficulty, we load the concrete victims into the station wagon and take them back to La Creuzette.

The police found the statues in the forest outside Lépaud, about 19 km from Boussac. A group of Gypsies had camped there for the night. Judging by the rubbish, and the empty wine and brandy bottles that had been left behind with the ruined statues, it must have been quite a party.

The Gypsies must have been overcome with joy to have found the two 'antique bronze figures', and at the thought of how much the brocanteur was going to pay them for this precious bounty. How great the disillusionment must have been when, in the cold light of day, they discovered that the statues were made of lowly concrete.

He who laughs last, laughs longest.

It takes me a few weeks to erect the statues again. They actually look more authentic now than they did before. The armless Diana now competes with the Venus de Milo in the Louvre. Every time I pass them on the way to the village, I greet my bronze gods with a wry chuckle: 'Salut, mes amis!' (Hello, my friends!)

Hardy wants me to show him where the nomads mutilated our classical gods. We follow my directions to the turnoff to the place in the forest where the Gypsies made camp. Once there, Hardy ignores my continual protestations and turns into an overgrown forest road.

'What is it with you? Have you got no ears?' My voice is thunderous.

'Wait and see. What I'm about to show you is far better than an empty Gypsy camp. Look!'

Between the trees, we see the spire of a château that's fallen in on itself. We drive closer, get out of the car. Right in front of the spire, a gnarled plum tree is putting on a spectacular show of its first blossoms.

'It's abandoned,' Hardy sighs.

We scan the area. Between the chestnut trees, we spot an impressive hunting lodge on the edge of a mysterious forest. Something stirs deep inside – a feeling somewhere between wonder and covetousness.

'I'll find out from the town hall whether it's on the market,' Hardy says. The sweep of his arm takes in the field of red poppies as if he's already its lord and master.

'No!' I bellow. 'One château is all I can handle! We're not even close to finishing La Creuzette, and already your eye is wandering!'

We drive back to La Creuzette in silence.

# 8

## Oh puh-leeze!

The moment before you lose all hope in the endless months of the French winter, late March brings a miracle. The French spring begins – something completely different from the one-act show in South Africa. Here, spring is a gradual awakening, delicate and full of nuance.

La Creuzette's garden is masterfully planned to display the spring at its very best. The first signs of new life are the stretches of snowdrops that appear everywhere under the trees. They glimmer in the gentle sun. The French call them *perce-neiges*: literally, 'snow-piercers'. Next, it's the turn of pools of yellow, purple and white crocuses, with their thick golden stamens and abundant saffron filaments. Then the daffodils and narcissus make their appearance, followed by the bluebells. By this stage, the trees are stirring, and the first tender green leaves of spring cautiously unfold.

Now the people of the countryside also leap into action. Shutters and hatches are thrown open; the more adventurous cover over the faded colours of the previous year with a fresh coat of paint. Rugs are beaten, crystal chandeliers are washed, and copper pots are polished for summer dishes.

Old men with bent backs are in the potager before daybreak.

They turn the soil in their vegetable patches in neat rows, and harvest the first rhubarb and asparagus. The two best spring dishes conceivable to me await. I can think of nothing better than the delicate flavour of freshly baked rhubarb tart with a dollop of crème fraîche. Or the first asparagus spears, steamed quickly, with a hollandaise or beurre blanc sauce. But at the very top of the list is a handful of grass-green wild asparagus, blanched and served with a knob of fresh butter. Merveilleux!

We, too, are busy sorting things out, and are planning the installation of a slew of new bathrooms. The bidets have to go. Loïc Delbard, our ungainly plumber – a short, stocky fellow with eyes that bulge a little and breath like ripe Camembert – is summoned.

Loïc is always ready with a joke or two, and his admiration of the female sex is legendary. He causes a bit of consternation when he gropes the derrière of one of our friends from Paris on our stairs. Sharp words are exchanged.

'C'est la fin des haricots!' I think our friend is asking for more of the green beans from last night's meal, but what she really means was that this is the last straw.

Loïc feigns innocence, and laughs his way up the stairs: 'Arrête ton char, madame!' This I know means something like 'Knock it off, lady,' She tilts her chin even higher than usual, and leaves in an icy fog. Back to civilisation.

The chambre de madame is first on our list. We have a beautiful ball-and-claw bath installed. I paint fantastical landscapes with trees and peacocks on the walls while the plumber installs a new toilet and basin in the water closet. It's strange to work in such close proximity to him; his risqué jokes are a good way to start the day.

When the clock strikes noon, everything screeches to a halt. The workmen lay down their tools, tongues flapping about the meal that is to follow. For the next two hours it is all eating and drinking, and nothing on earth will disrupt this centuries-old ritual. Whoever dares intrude on this holy observance soon realises that it's better just to pop into the nearest bistro yourself for a quiet meal.

I've been dressed down about this myself. Once, I nearly break my neck to rush into a shop just before midday. Wearing the smile of the victor, I point out to the monsieur what I want. He looks me squarely in the eye and says, politely, 'Bonjour, monsieur,' then adds, as evenly, 'Bon appétit' and 'Au revoir.' Without serving me.

I turn on my heel and stride, instead, to the nearest bistro. *Asperges sauvages avec sauce hollandaise* (wild asparagus with hollandaise sauce), *poulet rôti au citron* (roast chicken with lemon), *pommes de terre nouvelles* (new potatoes) and a wonderful *tarte à la rhubarbe* (rhubarb tart) are on the menu. The tart is so delicate; the ginger sauce is too delicious, with a spoonful of crème fraîche. It will be a few minutes, still, before I can tackle the monsieur behind the counter again, so I order a coffee. A noisette: a flavourful espresso with the tiniest shot of cream, just enough to make it nut-coloured. Hence the name.

We've learnt, by now, to enjoy our coffee black, and small – and that it's only the foreigners who order the café au lait grand crème. It's always made with yesterday's reheated dregs, served especially for the tourist with lots of milk and sugar. Locals and the enlightened have *un petit noir* set down before them, fresh and steaming. Vive la France!

Loïc the plumber rubs his puffy hands together in satisfaction. The new bathrooms are finally ready. I cannot wait to consecrate the whole lot of them, one at a time. It goes well; everything works exactly as it should.

The next morning is sunny and beautiful, a lazy Sunday morning with croissants and coffee in bed. After dispatching my petit déjeuner and testing the new bathroom installation, I throw open the double windows and gaze lovingly over the grounds. The garden is a real piece of paradise. But then I look down, and my eye settles on an unfamiliar sight. A fetid swamp is bubbling up between the irises – a hideous mess, complete with chunks of toilet paper.

I bolt down the stairs to investigate. When I'm a few paces from the scene, the smell confirms my worst suspicions. The brand-new bath, and other bathroom facilities, are connected to the antique French drain system. After just one use, it's overflowing.

'S'il vous-fucking-plait!' I scream at Loïc. This ancient septic tank arrangement is impossible to live with. We need to make a plan. Immediately.

Loïc tells us that the only solution is to link our bathrooms to the village's sewerage system. Since the house is in the middle of the grounds, all two hectares' worth, there'll need to be protracted digging, but Loïc will seek the mayor's permission and find a contractor to supply a quote.

When the contractor comes to deliver the quote, which is as long as my arm, Hardy is genuinely shocked. 'There is *no* way I'm paying that much for sewerage pipes. I'd rather dig the trenches myself – with a teaspoon!'

The contractor lights another Gauloises Blondes and gazes into the distance as if he's seen a spaceship. He leaves a little later, tail between his legs; he can see these Boers are not amused. On his way out, he tells us that it's solid rock where we need to dig – which is why his quote is so high.

Merde!

Luckily we have a friend with a (tiny) front-end loader. We decide to take our chances. When we've received the mayor's blessing, Hardy and our friend start digging.

First, the loader won't fit through the gate. With great difficulty, we take the back gate off its hinges. When our friend rolls the loader for the second time, Hardy takes over. In his zeal, he digs clean through a water pipe. For a split second the fountain is magnificent, then everything turns to mud.

Legend has it that La Creuzette is built on the site of a Roman market. When Hardy and the plumber eventually fix the water pipe, three pottery shards appear in the muddy trench. You can imagine our disappointment when the archaeologist in the village later informs us matter-of-factly that the shards are closer to Corningware than antique Roman pottery. This is the very archaeologist who spun us the yarn about the Roman market; every time he sees us, he asks in all earnestness when we plan to commence our excavations.

It turns out there is no rock to dig through after all; it's not long before we're connected to the village's sewerage system and can continue with the other bathrooms and the new kitchen.

We finish the digging just in time; soon afterwards the spring rains start to fall, and carry on for weeks on end. Loïc and his father work for days. On one specific day, they need to turn off the water supply so that they can replace some taps and fit the new kitchen sink. At midday on the dot, there's the customary laying down of tools and the exodus to go and eat. We must just not use the toilets, please, they request.

Hardy and I are busy on the top floor, also ready for a meal, the civilised Frenchmen that we are. We both need to go, but neither of us feels like braving the rain outside.

'Let's just wee in the basin, then go and eat. What harm could it possibly do?' I say, all self-satisfied.

We do so, and go downstairs for a nice lunch. The next minute I hear Hardy say, 'Oh hell!'

Loïc's blue metal toolbox is on the stove, concertina'd open, full of pliers and whatnot. A half-severed copper pipe hangs just above the toolbox: the drainage from the basin in the upstairs bathroom, which is right above the kitchen. It used to be connected to the sink's greywater pipes. One last drop falls into the toolbox with a plonk.

'No, jississ man, we peed in their toolbox!' I want to cry. 'What now?'

We spend the entire lunch break cleaning the toolbox, rinsing every tool, rubbing it dry and packing it carefully back into its place. Just in time: the two return, ready to get back to work. We greet them far too genially, and leave them in the kitchen with their gleaming toolbox. We're halfway down the passage when I hear Loïc say to his father, 'Strange guys, these South Africans . . . So friendly, and they even clean our toolbox while we're eating.'

'Bizarre,' the older man says. 'Bizarre.'

It will take a full five years for us to be able to open the doors of La Creuzette to guests. One of our projects was to appoint one of the outbuildings with a state-of-the-art kitchen and dining room.

This stately red-brick building once stabled six horses, and had two large areas for storing coaches and traps. It's a large building with storerooms, saddle and tack rooms, and a few other rooms, which we want to turn into sculleries and cold rooms. The attic, where the hay and feed were stored in winter, will become my studio. It's covered in centuries of dust, and is home to a squadron of spirited bats.

We try to do as much as possible ourselves, since the budget takes centre stage. The most significant change to the outbuildings is the new floor that the studio needs. The existing floorboards are very precarious.

I am down in the tack room one day when I hear a crack and, a moment later, Hardy's hoarse 'Help! Come here. Where are you?' And then, even louder, 'Bring the bloody ladder!'

I put down my saw and go to investigate. A set of flimsy wooden stairs leads upwards; there, between heaven and earth, I see Hardy's legs sticking out of the yellowed ceiling. Both of his legs have gone almost completely through the roof. He's still wearing one takkie. The other one has fallen off.

It takes me a while to track the ladder down. The gardener and I actually have to cut Hardy loose from the roof. Afterwards, all three of us are ashen from shock and dust; when Hardy wants to be pretentious he now puts on a limp, especially after he's embellished the story in the retelling of it.

The old people say that bad things happen in threes. Not long

Restoration projects require courage, hard work and a whole lot of luck. Here, Hardy tackles the wallpaper.

*Opposite:* The before photo of La Creuzette's sitting room.

*Below:* The front-end loader rolled twice while we were laying the sewerage pipes.

after Hardy's ceiling antics, we forget, that winter, to drain the pipes. When you close up your house for the winter in France, you're supposed to run all the water pipes dry and set the heating inside the house to *hors gel* (the frost-protection setting). This you *must* do, every year. But we're in such a hurry to get to South Africa that we completely forget to do it.

It's only when we unlock La Creuzette's elegant front doors a good few months later, full of life after a long summer holiday, that we take in the full extent of the catastrophe. The pipe in the bathroom of the main bedroom has burst, because the water inside it froze solid during the winter.

Water has seeped through the floorboards and the ceiling. The sitting room, or *grand salon*, directly beneath the bedroom is in terrible shape. The carpets are soaked, and the ceiling is full of huge blisters. Some have already burst; others just keep dripping, patiently. Wallpaper panels hang listlessly from stringy licks of glue.

The cherry on the cake is seeing how high the water has been soaked up on the silk curtains. Knee height. La catastrophe! Or, rather, la calamité, or le désastre. Which all comes down to the same thing: a complete disaster.

## 9

# A leg of lamb in a sock . . .

Restoring La Creuzette was not all just pain and suffering, though. This particular louis d'or coin – Louis XIII's predecessor to the Krugerrand – had another side, too.

When the restoration work is almost finished, it's one of the loveliest things to start on the interior decorating. We research the Napoleon III style and realise that it's one of France's most eclectic decorative styles. It fits me like a glove: I like mixing and matching. I mean, how exciting is putting a curved-glass coffee table in front of a gilded Louis XVI couch, with a Savonnerie carpet beneath it pulling the whole picture together?

There's a lovely story about the name and origins of the hand-knotted Savonnerie carpets. The mid-17th century was the golden age of the expensive Turkish carpet. So the French government decided to create a home-grown product that would satisfy the covetous French aristocracy. The first big carpet factory was an erstwhile soap factory (*savon* is the French word for soap) in Chaillot, Paris. These carpets, *à la façon de Turquie* (made in the Turkish way), became collectors' items in a flash, especially when the government banned the import of carpets from the Ottoman Empire and the East. Initially, Turkish and Persian designs were copied, but over time an authentic Savonnerie style evolved. These luxury wool and silk carpets consist of decorative medallion patterns and extravagant floral bouquets, framed by repeating ornamental bands. Exquis!

Hardy and I scratch around in antique shops and drive for kilometres in pursuit of brocantes. We attend auctions and public sales from Paris to L'Isle-sur-la-Sorgue in Vaucluse. We get to know the countryside at the same time. Hardy becomes a carpet, tapestry and Baccarat crystal aficionado. As for moi, I learn to spot Christofle silver from a mile away. I like interesting pieces, such as the antique Limoges porcelain portrait plates and polychrome parrots.

Another thing that Hardy has a weakness for is crystal chandeliers. La Creuzette needs almost two dozen of them, and he is on a mission. Remember, though: the sharp-eyed predator that is the budget is watching our every move.

We were in an antique shop, once, in a neighbouring village, each of us dizzied by our own object of desire. Mine was an 18th-century butcher's block that would fit our kitchen perfectly.

'Hardy, look – this block is just right for the kitchen,' I say. He saunters over and takes the price tag in his hand.

'No, man, it's too expensive. You've clearly forgotten that we have a budget,' he grumbles.

He walks back to where his desire – a glittering crystal chandelier – hangs like a wisteria from the roof. I head for the door, but he calls me back in.

'This is the perfect chandelier for the entrance hall,' he says, pointing at the roof.

'How much is it?'

'Not that much. We'll just have to cut things a bit fine for a month or two.'

'Oh,' I say, indignant, and start heading back to the door. 'I thought our budget didn't allow?'

'Wait, man. I've got an idea. I'm going to ask the owner to give us a good price if we take both. Clever, hey?'

I start laughing out loud: I know Hardy when he starts negotiating. I go and open the boot in the meantime.

Restoring La Creuzette teaches us so many new skills and loves. I can now plaster a wall, for example, if I have to. And we've both learnt so much about French cuisine: every few weeks we work with chefs from all over the world, which keeps us on our culinary toes.

But it's Hardy's knowledge of, and love for, tapestries that becomes the most exciting and enriching addition to our lives. It all starts with our first few visits to Aubusson, just down the road from Boussac. Good friends of ours own a factory that restores and manufactures tapestries. It's here that we learn the A to Z of weaving.

Aubusson is the cradle and capital of France's rich and fabled history of tapestry. It's usually the first destination on our guests' itinerary, and Hardy must surely be the most passionate tour guide: he knows every knot and stitch of most of the works in Aubusson's tapestry museum.

Soon enough, Hardy starts restoring our own large and growing collection of 17th- and 18th-century wonders himself. He goes to learn from one of the masters, and now has a collection of colourful spools that give my tubes of paint a run for their money.

Hardy finds tapestry auctions irresistible, so it's not long before every available space in the bedrooms, passages, hallways and salons is hung with his masterpieces. There's even a wonderful piece on the wall in the lounge of our holiday home on the West Coast – a 17th-century work called 'Summer'.

We befriend a generous young French trader and second-hand furniture seller. His name is Henri Aubert, and his shop is in an enormous watermill on the banks of the Tardes River near the spa town of Néris-les-Bains. An impressive Roman aqueduct, built in the 1st century AD, nonchalantly crosses a dry ravine just behind Henri's chamber of treasures.

Henri's lover is a fiery Spanish redhead. They fight a lot, so he often has to go and fetch her from her parents in Granada. After each romantic retrieval, Henri brings a load of antique Spanish furniture back to his watermill. We're at the top of the list of contacts he calls on his return.

This is how, one day, we stumble upon a beautiful hand-carved armoire. It takes seven men to carry the huge piece of art up the stairs at La Creuzette. When we show our guests to their rooms, we linger first at the armoire. We open the doors ceremonially to reveal layer upon layer of neatly starched antique linen sheets that we've collected over the years. It is without a doubt the loveliest and most photographed linen cupboard in all of France.

Good-quality beds and couches are extremely pricey, so we import the beds for ten rooms from South Africa. And, at Hardy's insistence, a fleet of industrial-sized Speed Queen washing machines, which he installs like superheroes in a neat row in the basement. This demonstrates his foresight: without these washing machines, and the *femme de ménage* (housekeeper) to run them, we would never be able to handle the bedding and table linen for the steadily increasing flow of guests.

We inherit our first housekeeper, Madame Deville, along with the few pieces of furniture that the duchess's family leaves for us. The minute our first bathroom has been redone and the entire house is covered in dust, Madame Deville decides to retire. Overnight.

After a few weeks of anxious searching, our friend Françoise brings Martine Emery to La Creuzette. It's love at first sight. We appoint her immediately. Almost two decades later, she is still the boss of all things French. Martine can do literally everything, from fixing a leaking tap to making a set of beds in record time while the guests drink tea in the salon, oblivious, and enjoy one of Martine's macaroons.

As La Creuzette starts to transform, so the number of friends who come to visit steadily increases. Some have an artistic streak, and come to help us with paint techniques on the newly finished walls. Others come to plant row upon row of lavender and rose bushes. Some come purely for moral support, drinking our cellar almost dry in the process. Funny how the best bottles always run out first.

'There's no more Châteauneuf-du-Pape,' says the wine snob, his upturned palms beseeching.

'Choose something else,' I say firmly. 'There's lots to choose from.'

'But I feel like Châteauneuf-du-Pape.' He looks tearful.

'The bottle store is downtown. Just take your credit card and ID with you.'

'Never mind. A Bordeaux will have to do. What's for lunch?'

Voilà! La Creuzette's newly renovated sitting room.

Hardy gives a musical performance in the
garden at La Creuzette.

*Opposite, above:* La Creuzette's dining room
with restored Aubusson cartoons
on the walls.

*Opposite, below:* Hardy's passion is tapestries.

One day, a friend who is also an accomplished chef suggests getting a few friends together and bringing them on a culinary tour. A garden fundi brings a group to view the most beautiful gardens in France. Another friend brings a group of friends to paint irises.

This is how La Creuzette's themed tours develop. Many of our guests come to paint, to write, to cook or just to experience the French lifestyle. The French call their unique way of life *la vie française* – something that they believe is specific to France. They may have a point.

The weeks become months, the stately La Creuzette comes into its own, our French vocabulary grows, and our sentences gradually lengthen. With an improvement in my French comes a new self-confidence. Cockiness, as Hardy calls it. Cheekiness, my father would say. There's clearly improvement, but my pronunciation keeps giving me trouble, no matter how many times a day I sing along with the fine Françoise, while Hardy gets the hang of French grammar with little effort.

It's the damn double entendres that still keep tripping me up. I will never forget asking the butcher, quite confidently, for a 'leg of lamb in a sock'. I look up the word 'deboned' on Google Translate, then blurt out my version of 'désossé'. What comes out of my diligent mouth instead is something like 'de chaussette'. The thickset butcher wipes his bloody hands on his blue-and-white-striped apron, informs me ruefully that 'You'll find socks in the shoe department,' picks up his enormous cleaver and hacks a rabbit carcass in half.

On another occasion, Agnès, an elegant friend from Paris, comes to spend a weekend with us. On the Saturday afternoon, we go to a small farm outside the village. Monsieur Dubois is a chicken farmer, and I am looking for a few hens. I want to introduce Agnès to the elderly couple, and stitch a longish sentence together to the best of my ability: 'Je voudrais bien introduire Madame Agnès Blondel.'

I'm quite proud of my beautiful, long French sentence. I stand back, broad-chested, but smell trouble when Agnès elbows me hard in the ribs.

Madame Dubois flinches. Monsieur Dubois clears his throat and says, 'Ah, bon!'

Very quickly and very loudly, Agnès starts speaking in beautiful French as she leads the madame away by the arm. The monsieur and I go off to the chicken coop. Every so often I catch him looking at me archly from under his bushy black eyebrows.

The moment we leave the farm, Agnès sets things straight. In French, you 'présente' someone. 'Introduire', which sounds so much like the English 'introduce', means to insert or penetrate – making what I said to the farmer and his wife unbelievably rude. I'm amazed the monsieur still sold me a few hens!

We wet the roof in earnest when the last new roof tile has been laid. The first paying guests are due shortly afterwards.

The opening is quite the affair. When the gilt-edged invitations land in postboxes exactly 14 days before the event, it sets the whole village abuzz. Hardy delivers those of the ten guests of honour in person.

Municipal workers erect a marquee in front of the new summer kitchen. For days on end, we starch and iron tablecloths and serviettes, and set tables. I've only got enough Christofle cutlery for two of the twelve tables, so I decide to make each table setting different. Each table has different plates, glasses and decorations. Necessity can be creativity's compost.

There are handwritten name cards in beautiful crystal holders next to every water glass. When the flowers are set out on the round tables, I know we've created something to be proud of. We continue to build on these high standards at La Creuzette.

Hardy outdoes himself by hanging three crystal chandeliers in the wild chestnut trees in front of the tent. What a sight to behold when they're switched on – a star-strewn piece of heaven in each tree. Before our guests take their seats, they each receive a glass of champagne in the hallway, its walls the colour of smoky quartz. The strains of Chopin's nocturnes issue from the music room.

The mayor proposes a high-flown toast. The French have a peculiar word for a housewarming: they call it a 'pendaison de crémaillère', a term from the Middle Ages that refers literally to hanging something on the chimney hook. People used to hang their cooking pots on this hook. The different notches allowed them to raise or lower the pot, regulating the cooking temperature. Clever, no? When you made the first pot of food in your new house, you warmed the entire room – hence the idea of a housewarming.

We must have made a good impression on the townsfolk, who welcome these two Boerseuns into the local community with no further ado. We're invited to just about everything, and we take part in everything that's on offer. We also make the grounds of La

Creuzette available for certain charity functions: picnics, big-screen movies and, yes, even a rock concert!

Hardy and I are united in our preference for classical music. Not because rockers are too wild, but because the dogs' ears can't handle the noise. At least he and I both have good earplugs.

I don't entirely agree with the old saying that we learn from our mistakes. In France, we learn, rather, through grit and daring. As the sand trickles through the hourglass, we work our very own foothold into the French countryside.

# 10

# Napoleon and Josephine

Four days after her 40th birthday, Elizabeth's husband says his goodbyes. Out of the blue, he takes the high road – the stony road that leads him away from their farm. Every now and then she'll refer to that day with a wry half-smile, then get back to her farm work, resigned. Her hands are rough and chapped, the look in her eyes one of purpose. Those eyes: they're disconcertingly blue, the colour of the Wedgwood china from her home town in England.

After a few hard years, the French farming community eventually starts to accept the British loner. Today, she is known for her organic farm products – the taste and quality of her lamb, in particular. She escorts the sheep on foot to the nearest abattoir, a journey of seven kilometres, believed to be one of the reasons why the meat she produces is so juicy and flavourful.

Elizabeth is devoted to her animals. Their care fills her days; there are rabbits, chickens, a cow with a calf, and two huge draught horses. And peacocks. Over 50 of them.

There are peacocks everywhere in her farmyard. On the farmhouse roof, on, around and in the barn, in the orchard. Brightly coloured peacock tails hang in bunches from the oak trees. The exotic birds' unsettling cry can be deafening at times, and can catch you unawares, filling you with a strange melancholy.

We're all of the opinion that some peacocks will add to the beauty and ambience of our garden. Elizabeth herself catches the pair that's destined for La Creuzette. While I'm helping her to load the birds, she tells me how she lured them into the kitchen before sunrise using bits of baguette she'd rolled into balls.

We decide to call them Napoleon and Josephine. It's quite a process to relocate the two peacocks to our temporary *pigeonnier* (dovecote), which has a small trellis-enclosed front yard and a chapel. (Yes, a chapel – this odd little structure is a miniature prayer or meditation room that's only big enough for one person.) The area enclosed by the trellis is covered with shade netting. For the peacocks' five-week reorientation period, we've put straw inside the chapel.

The time soon comes to set Napoleon and Josephine free. Elizabeth is there for the big event; she's even put on a dark-blue woollen suit for the ceremony, which she wears with a linen blouse that has a beautifully embroidered collar. I swear I even catch a whiff of perfume.

Napoleon is the first to hop out of prison. He fans his magnificent tail. While he struts, Josephine follows his lead. She hops right up to our feet, looks at us for a moment with a slightly cocked head, and flies with a soft whoosh up to a low branch in one of the nearby trees.

Her second attempt is a commanding flight – right over the wall. We watch as she vanishes into blue sky. We take off, calling after her. Napoleon keeps rustling his fantail.

We give up trying to find her just before midnight. We've called ourselves hoarse. The search will have to resume first thing tomorrow. For now, she's gone.

A while later, our neighbour tells us that she noticed a huge bird on the roof of her stoep on a dark night. She got such a fright, and yelled so loudly, that her husband sprang out of bed and rushed to investigate. He described the creature as a peafowl. She hopes this helps, she says.

Sébastien, our gardener, is certain the neighbours have caught Josephine for the pot. Peacocks and swans have been a delicacy for the French aristocracy since time immemorial. Vive la différence!

We also get two borzois during this time. Napoleon has to stand his ground against them; he takes to roosting on the roof of my studio. From there, he can watch over the whole village; in the dying moments of night, he announces the dawn and laments his long-lost love. The rooster in the chicken coop often then has his say.

Our two borzoi tenors are fond of launching into duets of their own. Ton and Anet are good-natured about the dawn chorus, but judging by the bags under their eyes, the nights are not the easiest. I suspect they buy earplugs by the bagful from Madame Martin, the pharmacist. I top up my own stock on the sly.

For entertainment, or perhaps from a deep longing for others of his kind, Napoleon courts the hens by day. The rooster is livid, and lets everyone know it. The hens, on the other hand, think nothing of the strutting and tail-fanning and peck away calmly at all that is earthworm and mielie.

From time to time, a lonely homing pigeon keeps Napoleon company. What a peculiar sight: a pigeon that thinks he's a chicken and a peacock that thinks hens are hot!

We hear later that Napoleon visits our neighbours three doors down and dispatches all their new lettuce and cabbage seedlings. He is apparently besotted with young tomatoes. And also, now and then, with flower buds.

I've barely taken my earplugs out one morning when a blood-red Madame De la Motte, the owner of said vegetable garden and flowers, starts hammering on the front door. Her flimsy dressing gown battles to conceal her ample bosom. When she waves her arms to emphasise the seriousness of the matter, I catch a glimpse of the milky-white peaks of Mont Blanc. And I'm not talking about skiing.

She has a formidable mouth. After half an hour or so she starts to calm down, allowing me to steer her back to the gate with a friendly but firm hand. I swear solemnly that we will take the peacock back from whence it came.

So it is that I instruct Sébastien later that morning to catch the peacock. On Thursday, I'll have to buy dozens of lettuce, cabbage, tomato and carrot seedlings at the market so that Madame De la Motte's dear husband can replant his potager from scratch. When the poor gardener has tried a good few times to catch Napoleon with the pool net, he tells me, out of breath, 'Peacocks cannot fly in the dark!' Who am I to argue? He announces that he'll come back later to catch Napoleon when the bird has settled on the roof. That I must have a piece of brioche ready.

That evening, Sébastien arrives fully kitted out for the hunt: boots, fingerless gloves, a kind of miner's torch fastened to his forehead. All he needs are a few diagonal black stripes on his face to be mistaken for Rambo. He climbs carefully out of the skylight with his net and stalks the peacock like a true soldier. From the garden, I see him crawl closer, Napoleon frozen in the glare of his head torch.

Sébastien was wrong: peacocks fly quite well, actually, in the dark. We throw in the net and go to bed, but not before I've worked my bright-yellow earplugs deep into my ears.

This time it's a hysterical Monsieur De la Motte who rounds on Hardy on the phone just after daybreak. Hardy doesn't even open his eyes; he simply stands there, shaking his head as he listens. I can hear the whole conversation through my earplugs. Monsieur De la Motte threatens us with the police and snarls all sorts of unpleasantries at us.

Later, we go down to Brigadier Dumas's office. We ring the bell. Many minutes later, an indolent voice asks us what we want. Yes, he says, Monsieur De la Motte has come in a few times already, and has recently voiced his suspicions about our peacock telephonically. He suggests that we seek the advice of *les pompiers*, the team of firemen that is mandated to solve problems in the village, and thank you for your cooperation.

Two plucky firemen meet us in our garden soon afterwards to make Napoleon's acquaintance. Each one has a long stick with a noose at the end. It's clearly going to be dead easy to catch a rogue like Napoleon with one of these. All day, the pompiers run back and forth across the yard, climbing up and down ladders, while Napoleon simply shuffles from roof to tree. They can't win. Initially, the firemen find it funny, but by the end of the day I see one of them throwing a half-eaten pomegranate at him.

The next morning, it's both Madame and Monsieur De la Motte at our door. It's not pretty. Thankfully, they are both fully clothed.

Wieletjies, one of our dogs, puts his front paws over his ears and gives a few strange whining barks. When I think that things are about to get physical, I tell them in no uncertain terms that I will call Brigadier Dumas if they do not vacate our property immediately.

To crown it all, Napoleon swoops over them and splatters Monsieur De la Motte's Sunday trousers, which have been ironed to a shine. Monsieur gives a desolate werewolf howl, then turns around and swears at us in incomprehensible French, fists balled. His wife shadows everything he does, albeit a little out of step.

The police and the firemen suggest we speak to a vet. We ask Jean-Pierre, the vet, whether he could dart the damn bird, please, with something that will send him into peaceful sleep. Jean-Pierre snorts, asking if I want peacock blood on my hands. No, he says, he will anaesthetise the bird with chloroform. A few drops from the brown bottle on a slice of bread, and voilà!

Jan, Hardy's brother-in-law, is visiting us at the time. Beside a crackling fire, he hatches a plan to catch Napoleon. We Boere men will catch the peacock ourselves by rolling bread balls in chloroform to bait him. Jan will stalk the bird in the long grass, and pin him down using the net. His daughters will then wrap Napoleon in a picnic blanket, so that he can be taken back to his original home.

The next day is a hot summer's day filled with butterflies and bees, and we've had a few bottles of cold rosé. We lure the unsuspecting Napoleon with the bread balls and Jan leopard-crawls through the long grass towards him. Twenty minutes later, the peacock has eaten his fill and Jan hasn't moved. One of us approaches carefully. Jan is snoring away in the long grass.

Hardy and I try ourselves, but we're not that steady on our feet – from all the rosé and hot sun, perhaps. Napoleon flies straight back up to the studio roof, his tail a trembling fan behind him. Clearly, the dosage was too low.

The sun is getting low when we wake from our afternoon nap. We decide to give it one last try, with a double dose of chloroform. I prepare the bread; Hardy opens a fine Bordeaux. In 20 minutes at most, Napoleon will have fallen, like Sleeping Beauty, into a deep and peaceful slumber.

The Bordeaux is finished. Napoleon still roams free.

I'm desperate. I drown a piece of bread in the rest of the almost-full bottle of the sedative. Napoleon thinks it's Christmas: he pecks away at the doctored *souskluitjies* with abandon. Hardy opens another bottle of Bordeaux, to pass the additional 20 minutes' lead time. I'm anxious that I've given the peacock an overdose and soon there'll be a dead bird on my stoep. What is Elizabeth going to think?

I gulp my glass of red and watch Napoleon like a hawk. An hour and a half later, when we've had our last sips of wine, Napoleon is still standing. The same cannot be said for us; we've opened a third bottle of Bordeaux in total amazement. It's as if the peacock is performing for us, fan dance and all. Hardy launches a final baboon-spider leap at the strutting bird, in vain. Napoleon shrieks his thanks and flies calmly up onto the studio roof.

We hear Napoleon's love song for a few more days, and see him courting the hens. The De la Mottes are suspiciously quiet. Our days resume a measure of normality. Hardy maintains that Napoleon has earned the right to stay at La Creuzette, and to hell with everything else.

One morning, it's dead quiet. The peacock is nowhere to be seen. The next day is the same. And the next. Later that month, I'm sitting in the hairdresser's chair. He tells me he's heard that the peacock has been shot. He won't say who told him this. I'm sure it was Monsieur De la Motte; I try to ignore them whenever our paths cross in town.

Not long afterwards, I bump into a friend from the neighbouring village, Boussac-Bourg. She tells me something quite strange. A pair of peacocks has started nesting in a deserted ruin just outside the village. There was originally just a peafowl, but a few months later a peacock arrived. She tells me how lovely they are, but that they are driving people crazy with their noise and that the local gardeners are complaining about the seedlings they keep losing.

We decide to go and investigate that weekend. Just so we know. We desperately want it to be Napoleon . . . and his Josephine.

# 11

## Becoming Frencher than French

Like most villages in France, Boussac has a *panier* (basket) full of old-fashioned customs and traditions that have survived since the Middle Ages. Things are done the way they're done, and to hell with modern sensibilities; the French are that invested in their traditions.

There can be no better example than the signature that concludes a French business letter: 'Restant attentif à vos préoccupations, je vous prie d'agréer, Madame, Monsieur, Cher(e) Collègue, l'expression de mes sincères salutations' (Remaining attentive to your concerns, dear madam, sir, colleague, I ask you to permit the expression of my sincere greetings). None of this 'Yours faithfully' or 'Cheers' business. I must confess, I secretly love all this courteous hat-doffing.

Despite the well-loved national motto – liberté, égalité, fraternité – a hidden snobbishness, especially when it comes to station and class, still breaks the surface here and there. Hence, a duchess may have two calling cards in circulation, even though both would be beautifully printed in black copperplate on ivory-white cotton paper. One would announce her as Comtesse M. H. V. A. de Blah Blah, and the other simply as Madame M. H. V. A. de Blah Blah. The first would be given out to colleagues, family and friends, and the second to members of the working class and socialists. We've received both.

Shortly after our arrival at La Creuzette, Marie-Thérèse and Pierre Boulet knock on our back door (the front door is by invitation only). A black velvet Alice band holds her well-groomed hair neatly in place. He wears a maroon tie with his dark suit.

These two kind people have come to bid us welcome, as it behoves the good souls who live in small towns. Marie-Thérèse has baked us a tarte au citron. With lemons from her own orchard. We feel the glow of neighbourliness and goodwill, and are very much at home in our new environment.

Late the next morning, we're at the point of halving the last slice, to wash it down with a cup of Carte Noire, when our friend Françoise pops in for her weekly catch-up. She brings us up to speed about the goings-on in the village, and she and I talk endlessly about art and philosophy. She studied art herself in her day, and has an exhaustive knowledge of contemporary art and music.

Françoise tells us that Colette Valois wants to know why the two South Africans haven't come to introduce themselves yet. Madame Valois and her husband own a massive 15th-century castle in the area. 'Aikôna,' I say to Françoise, a hint of indignation in my voice. 'That's not how Boers do things.' Then, 'No, really,' I say, thinking aloud. 'Not *another* châtelaine in the village. I'm certainly not going from house to house – or castle to castle – with my hat in my hand, introducing myself.'

After the weekend, Françoise visits again. Exhaling a light-blue ray of cigarette smoke, she tells us that Madame Valois *really* wants to meet us, and that we could get together on middle ground somewhere for an aperitif. Françoise offers to be our host. After a few days of calendar ping-pong to settle on a date, all parties agree to meet on a neutral Wednesday just after seven.

It is love at first sight. Colette Valois is a dynamic woman with an irrepressible lust for life, a contagious laugh and a gift for repartee. She is fitted out in Hermès haute couture from head to toe – her favourite fashion house, I'll later learn. The jewellery she has selected for the occasion is meticulously coordinated. Antique and modern. Chopard and Boucheron. She observes our ensembles with the eye of an expert, every garment, watch, cuff link, belt, shoe and sock. I've prepared well, coercing poor Hardy into all of his designer regalia too. I'm so well appointed for the evening's close scrutiny that I'd pass with flying colours on the basis of my new underpants alone.

A few days later, we receive a handwritten invitation.

The inaugural dinner at her castle is a visual tour de force. A tablecloth of luminous orange silk hangs over the table edge at each end, running along the floor for about another three metres in both directions. Only the lengths of the table are set – seven on one side, seven on the other. The plates are antique Sèvres, handed down through the generations of the Valois family, which can trace its origins back to the 12th century. Each guest has an antique silver christening cup as a water glass. Two large crystal vases of Madonna lilies and branches laden with small orange clementines decorate the table. Like the ambience, the food and wine are magnificent.

When it's my turn to entertain Madame Valois, the load weighs heavily on my mettle. I've considered using every excuse in the book – making measles with the hairbrush, claiming whooping cough, a broken arm. No cookbook offers redemption; I end up with my mother's *Kook en Geniet.* I'll deconstruct Boere recipes and transform them into wonderful, choice, modern dishes.

A day or so before the meal, we go to Paris for business. Luckily, I can pick up a few treats in the City of Light to spruce up my menu: Échiré butter and sel gourmand from the Grande Epicerie in the Rue du Bac, see-through sugar cubes from Mariage Frères, white Ethiopian peppercorns from Izraël in the Marais, a boule de seigle from Poilâne, a ripe Brie from Alléosse and a selection of dark-chocolate truffles from Debauve & Gallais.

But my *coup de théâtre* is what I think is an extraordinarily clever culinary idea: a course of hand-shaped sushi flowers from Lenôtre in the gardens of the Champs-Élysées. It's of utmost importance to me that I show our French friends that we, too, have a bit of finesse when it comes to cooking and entertaining; most of them think our children ride to school on kwaggas and that we squat around the campfire to eat our daily bread.

The first course is a soup made from fresh green peas and baby spinach leaves, with a dash of crème fraîche spruced up with a hint of tonka bean and nutmeg. A golden-brown, miniature vetkoek accompanies it. Then, each guest is presented with a little round bobotie tower with a blood-red sweet chilli preserve sauce and a milk-white coconut liqueur in a liqueur glass.

A palate cleanser of plum eau de vie – plum witblits – follows.

Next is a beautiful plate displaying the three pieces of sushi from Paris – gorgeous, semi-transparent, rose-like tuna flowers, with one single wasabi rose. The jewel-like detail is astonishing. The pieces look like rare works of Oriental art, hewn from antique jasper. A masterpiece of Zen composition. It takes everyone's breath away.

I watch Colette Valois load the grass-green wasabi rose onto her silver Christofle fork, smile at the guest beside her, catch my eye and slip the little jewel between her red-velvet Dior lips. She swallows. It's as if time stands still. For a few seconds, nothing moves or makes a sound.

Colette swallows again. Her nostrils flare like those of a race-horse in the starting gate. Her mouth opens soundlessly, like Edvard Munch's figure screaming on the bridge.

Sound and movement suddenly return to the table. Glasses tinkle, there's swallowing and coughing, a few shrill dry sneezes. Benjamin, the waiter, is pouring litres of Evian for madame. She won't drink sparkling water – not even in an emergency.

Colette carefully dabs her eyes dry with her serviette, lightly wipes the corners of her red mouth and says in a hoarse little voice that everything is fine and that she likes sushi a great deal and could we all just carry on as normal, merci.

The main course is ostrich fillet with a red wine and chocolate reduction, oven-baked beetroot slices, broccoli puree and individual ginger jellies, quivering on the edge of the plate. The whole meal, including the cheese and desserts (one of which comprises individual little vinegar puddings with quince foam), plays out before me in a haze. It's only when the coffee, chocolate and fruit are served that the table comes back into focus.

Colette excuses herself and stays in the guest toilet for an inordinately long time. On her return, her lips and eyes are touched up to perfection; a whiff of perfume returns with her.

'I know sushi,' she says. It sounds like she's been breathing helium, but at least she's in control of her faculties again. She laughs, shimmering like the wealth of tiny stones on her bracelet. We're old allies now; I'm sure she's already planning her next dinner.

To this day, whenever Hardy and I mention that first dinner with Madame Valois, we say, simply, 'Puff the Magic Dragon', while I sing at the top of my voice, dancing with the broom as a partner: 'If you know sushi, like I know sushi ...'

Since Asterix's time, the French have been very proud of their hunting tradition. It's a national pastime. Weekends, especially Sundays, are set aside for it. Think very carefully before you go walking around in the forest between September and March – shooting accidents are an annual occurrence. If you absolutely have to go for a stroll, put on your bright-red bonnet and bellow your chanson repertoire as you go.

Wild boar and deer are the most popular trophies, with rabbit, pheasant and wood snipe also top contenders. Environmental groups try in vain to discourage people from hunting. Here, people hunt for the table, and anything that has to do with food is unimpeachable. Simmering stews, roasting joints and pâtés spread over thick slices of farm bread are the order of the day.

One of Duchess Marie Helene's children once visits La Creuzette, and brings his family with him. His eight-year-old grandson is eager to see what it looks like these days, and to look at the armoire in which his grandmother used to store all sorts of delicious treats.

After viewing it, the boy asks about the stone staircase that

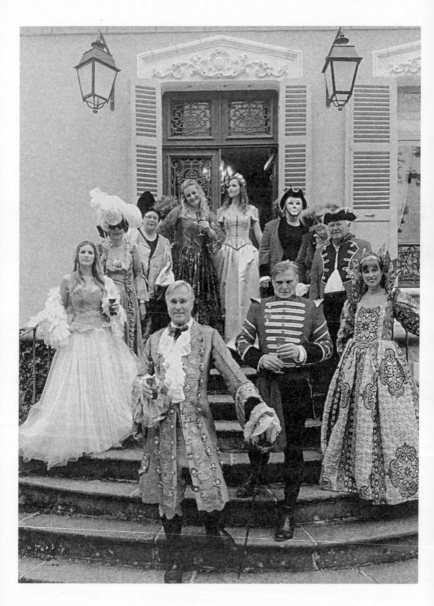

A dress-up party on Bastille Day.

On Bastille Day
we usually have
big celebrations
and also make
some music.

*Below:* An al fresco
lunch with Bella
Niehaus (top row,
far left) and some
of our guests.

leads to the cellars. When the children were naughty, their grandmother would frighten them with the story that a wild renard used to shelter there. The fox puts naughty children in their place, she would warn.

The father reassures the child, and the three of us descend the stairs. 'See? It was all just a story,' he says, and lets go of the child's clammy little hand. With that, August the borzoi emerges from his bed. For the poor child, this uncommon wolfhound, with his sharp snout and bushy tail, is far too close to a fox for comfort. He leaps into his father's arms.

A tonic for the tired hunter: slice a few nicely ripe apples, fry them in butter until they are golden brown, flambé them gently in Calvados and serve them with crème fraîche – and another tot of Calvados! Who knows? There could be a fox just around the corner.

Another important French tradition is La Fête nationale, Bastille Day, the most important folk festival in France. It's celebrated with great gusto on 14 July across the entire country – from Paris to Perpignan, Nantes to Nice, Strasbourg to Sète.

On 14 July 1789, the Parisians stormed the Bastille to free political prisoners in the name of the Republic. This prison was a much-loathed symbol of oppression by the tyrannical monarchy. The storming of the Bastille sparked the revolution, which is why it's commemorated as the birth of the French First Republic.

From the Auvergne and the Midi-Pyrénées in Languedoc-Roussillon to the Côte d'Azur, you'll hear, on this day, the compelling tune of 'La Marseillaise', the French national anthem:

Allons enfants de la Patrie,
Le jour de gloire est arrivé!

(Come, children of the fatherland,
The day of glory has dawned!)

'La Marseillaise' is an impressive combination of rousing lyrics and dramatic marching music. It's one of the many symbols that has its origins in the revolution.

On Bastille Day, a colossal Tricolore flies in the arch of the Arc de Triomphe. A massive brass band leads the military parade, bearing fluttering banners and pennants, down the Champs-Élysées – past the rows of plane trees and thousands of cheering spectators, all beneath a sea of blue, white and red flags.

Since it's high summer, and only gets dark properly at 10.30 pm, the celebrations are crowned with fireworks displays across the land. The whole performance reverberates with the revolution's inspiring motto – liberté, égalité, fraternité!

In the countryside, there is equally intense celebration. Brocantes, fêtes, agricultural shows and farmers' dances are arranged. In every town square, a colourful carousel whirls and joyful folk songs bubble forth from hand-painted barrel organs. At night, the grey stone churches are magically transformed into fairylands. Cheerful organ melodies mingle with the voices of carefree children; the scent of caramel and cinnamon hangs sweet and warm in the night air. Next to every lake and dam, bulky oxen and fat sheep turn on spits. The voices of revellers, and their antics, spill out of the brightly lit tents in which the food is served.

Boussac's Fête nationale gets equally spirited. A sizeable bro-cante is held in the town square, where Anet and Hardy are usually among the top sellers of the bric-a-brac they've been hoarding. One of our good French friends often tells the story of the huge bargain she got from these two: the ugliest cup and saucer imagin-able, from Woolies, with an awful yellow design around the edges. Her husband still has his tea in this fine English porcelain every morning, she tells us proudly. 'Oh la vache!' (You don't say!)

Anet once bought two ruby rings for next to nothing from a young schoolgirl. She only paid €5 per ring, I think. She had the rings valued in Cape Town. They had good stones, set in yellow gold. I swear the kid lifted the rings from her granny's Dolly Varden.

The village's fireworks display sometimes takes place in the gardens of La Creuzette. It takes days to set everything up; the dogs are especially fond of chewing the wooden frameworks for the larger rockets. Of course, we have our own Bastille Day dinner – a jovial mix of French and South African friends. The fireworks are usually timed for just after the main course. One of the organisers comes to warn us that the proceedings are about to get under way, and hurriedly switches off the lights.

In the distance, we hear the drums of the marching band. A moment later, the first few hopeful sounds of the pompiers' brass band filter through. They lead the townspeople from the town square to the iron gates of La Creuzette. Children with lamps glowing at the end of long sticks stare in anticipation at the dark, mysterious garden. They can only just make out the grey silhou-ette of the château. For a moment, everything falls silent. Then, cheeks bulging, the trumpet players strike up a vibrant fanfare...

the children's mouths gape, their hands groping for those of their parents.

The first golden flash shoots through the ink-blue heavens with an otherworldly hiss, exploding in a blinding rain of fire. Another, then another, streaks a brightly coloured stream of sparks past the treetops, opening a neon umbrella to the Milky Way. And now, from the dusky street, the unmistakable notes of 'La Marseillaise'. Like a fever dream, glowing lanes of blue, white and red sparks light up the façade of the château. The crowd's delight erupts into raucous applause. Vive la France!

Preparations for the Bastille Day party take days. Tables and chairs are moved out into the garden, and Hardy needs to wire up some crystal chandeliers in the chestnut trees. There's plenty of spit and polish. Crates of champagne are cooled. Chickens are deboned. Salmon is steamed pink in salty crusts.

Elegant and gracious, Anet is our hostess/high society lady who helps with everything – including keeping our guests happy. The party is a chance to dress up; one year, Anet's designer dress arrived in Boussac just in the nick of time – literally minutes before the first guests pitched up, far too punctually. When she put on the beautiful cream-coloured dress, the waistband slipped down to her knees. She had minutes to come up with a creative solution. Using satin ribbon in blue, white and red, she plaited a delicate belt, stylishly holding the intransigent waistband in place. Voilà, our very own Marianne!

Marianne is another beloved symbol of the revolution. She is portrayed as a beautiful but fearless woman who led the freedom fighters to the battlefield behind a fluttering national flag. She is the symbol of freedom, and of the innate power of the French woman. A bust of Marianne is found in every town hall and court building, and she is depicted in art as well as on postage stamps and official documents. French beauties such as Brigitte Bardot, Catherine Deneuve, Laetitia Casta, Inès de la Fressange and Vanessa Paradis have all served as inspiration for the Marianne figure.

For the first time since the 1920s, Boussac sports its own gilded Marianne figure on the town square. Her chin tilts upwards proudly to the north, and she looks out with a steady gaze towards the City of Light.

Once we've served the dessert and champagne, local musician Michel Bolling opens his piano accordion wide. He rocks as he plays, the songs clear enough to ensure that everyone soon starts singing along:

> Ah! Le petit vin blanc
> Qu'on boit sous les tonnelles
> Quand les filles sont belles ...

> (Ah! the white wine
> That we drink beneath the pergola
> When the girls are beautiful ...)

One by one, the couples, still singing, start dancing under the trees, swaying, twirling, filled with the sheer pleasure of living. The youngsters stand on the sidelines, wiggling their hips; two expats from London *langarm* through the harlequin flowers.

Hardy and Anet make a show of their foxtrot, weaving through the dancing couples, while I attempt a cotillion with the baker's pasty daughter. Simon, the blacksmith's precocious youngster, does an impressive fire dance at the herb garden's gate – with no ill effects, fortunately.

It's not until daybreak that Michel latches his piano accordion shut and settles it deep inside its maroon velvet case. La vie est belle …

# 12

# 'Chocolatl'

In France, the term of endearment for someone with a sweet tooth is *un bec sucré*, a 'sweet mouth', or *suikerbek*, as the Afrikaans has it. All French people are raised to become *suikerbekkies*, and know the difference between crème pâtissière and crème anglaise from the youngest age. Even eight-year-olds know their butter cream from their almond cream.

The French have a collective sweet tooth. Every day they indulge, choosing from an astoundingly large variety of confection. It's the land of the gourmet, where food is as important as politics or religion. Everyone philosophises about ingredients, taste, quality and presentation, and has an informed opinion about the wheres, whys, whens and with whoms of eating.

France's gourmandism has a long history. When Catherine de' Medici married Henry II in 1533, she and her entourage brought with them a mass of cooks, caterers and bakers from Italy. Her imported specialists rapidly developed exciting new recipes and dishes; in 1566, a new guild was born: the pâtissiers.

The development of puff pastry was a highlight of these times. Mille-feuille has been used in thousands of recipes as the foundation for the most exciting confection we know. The first French superchef, Antonin Carême (1784–1833), took it to new heights.

His pièces montées and croquembouches were complex, ornamental showpieces, often standing metres tall – entirely edible.

Jean-Anthelme Brillat-Savarin (1755–1826), the philosopher, lawyer, master gourmand and father of French haute cuisine, wrote *Physiologie du goût*, an important book about the psychology of taste. His famous maxim 'you are what you eat' is still regarded as a national subtext today. It is thanks to this remarkable approach to life that we have such an astonishing spectrum of delicacies in the world today; France's intense relationship with the art of eating and food preparation offers a glimpse into the complex French psyche.

Most villages have a *boulanger* (baker). There are three in Boussac. There used to be four, but the one who was best known for baking tarts was killed in a neighbouring village. A crime passionnel, people say from behind their lace curtains, chewing on the opposition's marzipan crocodile. Death by chocolate.

Luckily for us, the baker that is closest to La Creuzette is not only at the top of his game but is also a wonderfully talented tartmaker. He trained as a sous-chef in Paris, and conjures up the most imaginative cuisine in his kitchen. Flat cake, cream cake, layer cake, Swiss roll, fruit cake, fridge cake, sponge cake, you name it – in any colour and flavour.

Petits fours go into the oven when the larger cakes come out. They bake at a 'smaller' temperature, hence their name, which directly translates as 'little ovens'. They are served at chic French tables with the dessert, or after the meal with a petit noir. There'll also be a shot of something sweet, a Pineau or a chilled glass of yellow-gold Monbazillac.

In France, confection is mostly a Sunday thing. Orders are placed weeks in advance. There are families who have been placing the same bakery order every week for generations. The baker knows that Madame So-and-so comes in at just after nine for six framboisines – moist almond-flour tarts soaked in kirsch, filled with velvety butter cream, covered with a transparent strawberry-jam glaze and garnished with fresh, thinly sliced strawberries. And Madame This-and-that comes at just before half past for her weekly croissants and a dozen mille-feuille au framboise – crisp, golden-brown puff pastry tarts filled with crème pâtissière, topped with a layer of raspberry syrup and candied almonds. Monsieur So-and-so is ready at the counter like clockwork just before lunch every Sunday for his baguette and half a dozen madeleines.

If something about this paramount ritual goes wrong, the baker knows that his culinary misstep won't soon be forgiven. In Paris, people stand patiently in queues that go around the block to buy their weekly confection from centuries-old establishments such as Ladurée and Dalloyau.

Macaroons are ferried all over Paris in beautiful cardboard boxes tied with satin ribbons: chocolate with cognac cream, strawberry with peppermint cream, pistachio with white chocolate cream and, my hands-down favourite, caramel with honey and lavender cream. Larger boxes filled with cakes are carried out with both hands, cautiously and reverently. Inside them could be a square Opéra, a cake that commemorates the Opéra Garnier in Paris: layers of chocolate cake resting on a joconde biscuit crust, filled with coffee caramel and chocolate ganache, and finished with a layer of bitter dark-chocolate icing sugar. Or a gâteau coccinelle, a beautiful almond sponge cake, filled with pistachio ice cream. It's shaped like a giant ladybird, and covered in a smooth, shiny glaze with hard-pear syrup and chocolate spots. Magic!

The *galette des rois* (kings' cake) is a simple, flat, puff pastry cake made with almonds, vanilla custard and a decent shot of rum. It's an extremely popular cake, eaten all across France on Twelfth Night (la Fête des Rois). Because eating it is such a sweet business, it's usually served with strong black coffee or champagne.

The village bakers use all measure of gimmicks to compete for baking the biggest or loveliest Twelfth Night cake. As do the supermarkets, which make dozens of these cakes in eight different

The kings' cake.

sizes. Their extravagant window displays stop passers-by in their tracks. Children and adults alike are enchanted, then enticed: the delicious treat is sold with an endearing gold crown.

Traditionally, a game is played when the galette des rois is eaten – before it is baked, a small porcelain tile or figurine is concealed inside it. After the meal, the cake is divided evenly among the guests. Whoever finds the little toy in his or her slice of cake is crowned king of the day or evening. King Whomever then opens the dance floor at the head of a conga line, towing all the slightly sulky guests behind him or her.

Our first Twelfth Night dinner at La Creuzette is a feast in more ways than one: time with new French friends, snow under the trees, crackling fires, the table groaning under the weight of winter dishes.

After the meal, the huge galette des rois is sliced, and each of the 12 hefty slices is served with a dash of crème fraîche. Guests use the miniature grater to grate a little nutmeg or tonka bean over their cream. We serve a glass of Beaumes-de-Venise, too.

As it behoves the good host, I dish up the last skew little piece for myself and tuck in.

Crack! My eyes suddenly start streaming: it's porcelain on porcelain . . .

I flee the table, candles guttering in my wake. The guests make rude noises; one actually starts filming me with his iPad. What is an iPad doing at the table in first place? I see I'm going to have to start leaving my etiquette book lying around again.

Ça ne va pas! (This is not okay!) The bathroom mirror confirms my worst suspicions – I am toothless. There are two pieces of porcelain in my hand: a man in a little blue hat, and my front tooth. There's nothing but a glistening nib where my pearly white eye tooth should be.

My desire to party evaporates there and then. After struggling for a good while to get the crown back in, I give up on the evening, right there in the bathroom. Lips pursed, I gesture to the restless guests that the party is over, and that they can forget about a group photo.

Hardy laughs himself stupid. A crown on my head and one in my hand, I descend my throne and storm off to bed. First thing in the morning, we head to the dentist in the van, which is still full of rubble and dust from our renovations. To keep up appearances, I'm holding the crown in place between my forefinger and thumb. The dust in the cab is horrendous. My nose twitches like that of a rabbit that can smell a carrot. I'm going to sneeze. There, in the almighty explosion of vapour, I see my crown flying through the air, hitting the windscreen and vanishing in the sand between my feet.

I blunder around for it for what feels like a lifetime; think needle-in-haystack. By the time I find it, the dentist has long since gone home, probably to scoff a piece of bloody kings' cake. I have to wait until Monday for help.

The bitterest pill? That night, I have to make a speech at a friend's wedding. I refuse to lisp my way through it; when I notice the bottle of superglue on the window sill, I know what I have to do. With a c'est-la-vie look in my eyes, I walk towards the sunny spot at the window.

What happens that night at the wedding is a story for another day.

It's not just confection for which the French have such a sweet proclivity. They are also chocolate experts.

Only in France is there an annual, countrywide, week-long, chocolate-celebrating festival each October. In Paris, it's called Salon du Chocolat. At designated tasting locations, the country's foremost chocolatiers – and, these days, those from other countries, too – uncover the very latest chocolate trends to the public.

Names like Lenôtre, La Maison du Chocolat and Debauve & Gallais vie for the attention of the public with exceptional gourmet chocolate displays. France's top chefs put forward the most exquisite flavours in a plethora of imaginative shapes and packaging: gold leaf, silver paper, candied violets, bright-gold mimosa balls. A few years ago, celebrity chef Jean-Paul Hévin designed a wearable chocolate wedding dress, compete with veil and train. At his shop on the Rue de Bretagne, the Chocolate Bar(re), one of the more adventurous snacks you'll find is a dark-chocolate ganache mixed with sheep's milk, Roquefort and Pont l'Évêque cheeses. This tells me that we South Africans may not be as backward as the French think we are: way back when I was in primary school in Middelburg, the kids next door were already making us sandwiches with cheddar cheese and melted Milkybar!

In 2019, the chocolate festival was dedicated to the bee. The continued use of insecticides the world over is threatening the survival of bees. The French have launched a range of wonderful initiatives to save the honeybee from extinction. In Paris, there are beehives on apartment roofs that have been there since 1856. Bees have always been welcome in this city. By 2016, there were over a thousand rooftop beehives in Paris. Today, the historical hives that have endured since the 19th century are nurtured with care, and with great public interest. There are even hives on the Palais Garnier's beautiful roof.

The highlight of the Salon du Chocolat has become the fashion show. A top French designer is invited to create a few designs using chocolate. Pale models then display them on the catwalk to a jubilant crowd; tickets to this glamorous event are sold out months in advance. You'd be completely amazed by the detail, texture and shape of these pieces of chocolate couture. Thank heavens it's already a bit cooler in October – and that there's air conditioning. Imagine the commotion if a festival like this were held in Pofadder in the middle of summer!

Then there are the many other chocolate happenings that are as popular, but a great deal more ... underground. In one of these, a naked model is painted with a delicious trio of white, milk and dark chocolate. When those spectators who have been able to come by a ticket, and who can afford one, arrive, they have a pot of luke-warm chocolate and a paintbrush thrust into their hands. Et voilà! Some of the more aesthetically acceptable results make their way to the back page of the newspaper. Some of these happenings get a bit out of hand, sometimes, with foreign body parts being dipped into the gleaming melted chocolate.

According to the history books, the Mayans were the first to combine chocolate and honey to make a thick, foaming drink, apparently enjoyed with every meal. It was the Aztecs who gave us the word 'chocolate', by blending *chikolli* and *āti* – in Nahuatl, these mean stake (or stirring stick) and water. Before long, we had the lovely word 'chocolatl'!

There are many stories about how the cocoa bean made its way to Europe, but the most plausible is that it arrived in Spain with Christopher Columbus in 1502. It was unattainably expensive for all but the rich and famous. As happens with most practically unobtainable luxuries, chocolate fever spread like wildfire through Europe. The Spanish in turn got chocolate from the Aztecs; so it was that it came to the royal court of France when it was given as a gift on Anne of Austria and Louis XIII's wedding day in 1615. It has been an institution in the French monarchy since that joyful day.

The story claims that François Massialot was the first French chef to use chocolate in his cuisine. His book, *Le Cuisinier Royal et Bourgeois*, refers to it as early as 1691. Incidentally, Massialot is also the father of crème brûlée and crème au chocolat, still firm favourites of many people today. Massialot would often throw a block of chocolate into his pot-au-feu, as is the custom today when making boeuf bourguignon. There, now you know the secret!

Today, the chocolate industry is strictly controlled, with the French claiming to be one of the world's foremost manufacturers – a claim that is supported by a few interesting facts. One of the world's most famous and respected chocolate manufacturers is Valrhona, whose factory is located on the Rhône River, south of Lyon. Valrhona uses only cocoa beans from the Criollo tree in its chocolate. These rare beans constitute a mere three per cent of the world's cocoa production. The rest of the world uses the Forastero bean, predominantly, which is more widely available and has a taste that is apparently a little less unique. The very best beans are sorted and roasted, very slowly, at Valrhona. As with the best wines from the Rhône Valley, there are specific blends, made according to colour, taste and texture.

French chocolate manufacturers are obliged by law to mix their cocoa powder with cocoa butter; the rest of the world uses plant-based oils instead. The French turn their aristocratic noses up at anything less; chocolate, they'll tell you, is – like wine, perfume and racehorses – a connoisseur's choice. There is as big a difference between a KitKat and a Debauve & Gallais as there is between Sea Cottage and a Bentley!

Debauve & Gallais's oldest chocolate boutique is on the Left Bank, in the Rue des Saints-Pères. This celebrated company has been the chocolate maker of the French monarchy since the reign of Louis XIII, but it was during the reign of Louis XVI that Debauve & Gallais earned worldwide renown. Marie Antoinette, the wife of the king, hated taking bitter medicine. So she instructed Sulpice Debauve, the royal pharmacist, to find an antidote to the bitterness. He made an ingenious chocolate coin that was both sweet and rich, sweetened with honey from Paris's rooftop bee-hives. The Queen was so taken by the coin that she convinced Debauve to make a whole series of them for her and her courtiers at Versailles. He called them Pistoles de Marie-Antoinette. They became immediately popular – so much so that the courtiers would go through large volumes daily. In 1913, Pistoles de Marie-Antoinette became available to the public. To this day, they are top sellers.

When you're invited to a formal French dinner, it's particularly endearing to surprise your hostess with a selection of Debauve & Gallais chocolates. These are still presented in the official royal packaging, with its impressive blue-grey and gold colouring. La Royale is an astonishing collection that has been served at special occasions since the reign of Louis XIV. Your hostess will be unbelievably impressed. Rest assured: guests will be lost for words when one of these treats lands on their tongues.

The large box – 76 petites délices – will set you back €515 (about R10 000). But hold your horses ... Royales also come in smaller boxes, containing as few as 12. And €38 is not *that* bad – it's only about R730. Granted, a bit more expensive than a pack of M&Ms.

Debauve & Gallais's shop in the Rue des Saints-Pères is worth a visit, even if all you can afford to do is gape at the mind-blowing variety and unbelievable craftsmanship of the delicate chocolate jewels. It's highly likely that you'll walk away with a bag of Emperor Napoleon Croquamandes. These were specially made for Napoleon Bonaparte: clusters of roasted almonds in caramelised sugar, swathed in a layer of slightly bitter dark chocolate. Tonight, Josephine!

If you're a chocoholic, best you master the following French words. Praline: a mixture of roasted almonds and hazelnuts caramelised in invert sugar. Ganache: chocolate mixed with cream and butter. Gianduja: roasted and ground hazelnuts and chocolate.

Pierre Hermé is one of Paris's best-known confectioners. His chocolate macaroons are double-chocolate rolls with a heavenly filling. Hermé's love for chocolate is legendary; he uses it with daring and commitment in most of his confection.

À la Mère de Famille in the Rue du Faubourg Montmartre is also worth a visit. This extraordinary shop's beautiful 19th-century façade is something to behold; it's been peddling chocolate since

1761, and still makes the famous Palet Montmartre: a wafer-thin chocolate disc filled with praline or ganache.

I've been a self-confessed chocoholic for some time, and part of my monthly therapy is a visit to Angelina in the Rue de Rivoli. It's nearly 120 years old, a meeting place for buzzing groups of friends to chatter away and be seen. The who's who of the avant-garde have been queuing here for coffee, tea and Angelina's famous confectionery since the 1900s. Writers, artists and politicians have made it a sought-after place: Proust and Coco Chanel are among the celebrities who used to be seen there almost every day.

Like the haute couturiers, Angelina presents a new confectionery range twice a year – with great fanfare. The 2019 spring/summer collection included the enticing Louise, among others: a piquant green tea, almond and strawberry tart that makes you see stars.

Angelina's world-renowned L'Africain has been on the hit list for decades. It's a thick, dark, steaming chocolate drink that's served with a little jug of fresh cream. It's the world's most famous hot chocolate, and should be at the top of everyone's wish list. According to tradition, you eat a Mont Blanc with it – a tart with a meringue base, filled with a sweet chestnut purée and topped with whipped cream. Heavenly! L'Africain makes this Africain feel right at home, even though French pronunciation still twists his tongue.

The French like telling jokes. Bad jokes, sometimes, but usually ones involving food or eating. 'What is a cat's favourite Christmas pudding?' Madame X asks me after a dinner at her watermill house on the Petite Creuse.

I shake my head, wiping my mouth after my last morsel of dessert.

'Chocolate mousse!'

Everyone laughs themselves to tears.

When I get to tell a very simple joke or story in French, they all thump me on the back and say, 'C'est une histoire très drôle' (What a funny story that is). Drôle: what a strange French word, I think to myself, in Afrikaans. Just keep it away from the drinking water, please!

# 13

## Not all frogs become princes

Paradise is not all princes and princesses; there is the occasional frog, too. Not all French people smell like Chanel No 5, and they are definitely not all amiable goody-two-shoes. As a character in Canadian writer Douglas Coupland's novel *Microserfs* says, 'We decided the French could never write user-friendly software because they are so rude.' This loaded pronouncement brings me to the topic of snooty French waiters. They are a breed of their own, known all over the world for their incivility – especially when the *blikskottels* see that you're an étranger. Then all you see is their nostrils.

Just try to catch a waiter's eye – I dare you. It's practically impossible. He will continue polishing that wine glass, the one that's already shining like the Milky Way. When he walks past your table, he turns his whole body in the opposite direction.

If you're stupid enough to click your fingers and squeal, 'Garçon!', like they do in American movies, it's all over for you. You might as well decamp to the bistro next door.

Remember, too, that there's a difference between a café, a brasserie, a bistro and a restaurant, and that each one has its own codes of behaviour and whatnot. You'd better go and google them, my friend. Otherwise you'll be knee-deep in the you-know-what. Again.

We are regulars at our favourite bistro in one of Paris's glass-roofed arcades. We've got to know the manageress well, as well as one of the waiters: Gilles, the bistro's oldest and sourest. Once, after an exhibition in London, and a journey back to Paris on the Eurostar, we are looking forward to a meal at our favourite bistro. We walk through the first dining area, which is filled with patrons. Glasses tinkle and forks clink on white porcelain plates. We greet the manageress, who is busy helping a woman out of her coat. I can smell the wave of perfume from where we are patiently standing and waiting. The manageress gestures to us to go through to the second dining area. To Hardy I say smugly, 'Good to be home.' You know you've 'arrived' in France when you're recognised – and acknowledged – in a well-known Paris bistro.

The second dining area is large – it must have over 40 tables. A Frenchman of ample proportions – Shrek's very own cousin – is eating at one of the tables. He's tucked his serviette into his collar; his mouth shines like the evening star with smears of duck fat and mushroom sauce. His partner is not much smaller. Their bodies literally overhang the table next to theirs. Her large Dior tote yawns open on the chair beside her.

Gilles stands guard at the entrance. I clear my throat to greet him with a genial 'Bonsoir, Gilles.'

Before I go on, let me express my amazement at the French fascination with small things. I'm not talking about shiny Cartier stones or crystal Balenciaga bottles. I'm talking about Paris's small living spaces and tiny lifts. Incroyable! (Unbelievable!)

It's the miniature bistro and restaurant tables that floor me, though. They're seldom bigger than 60 x 60 cm for two, and only a fraction bigger for four and six. But watch all hell break loose if the two of us go and sit at a table for four. To crown it all, the tables are always pushed right up against each other.

I recall once sitting at a table on the pavement outside a chic bistro, next to a neat little couple. The waiter had hooked our wines, in their beautiful silver wine coolers, onto our tables. Because our two tables were so close to one another, the bottles were hanging in the gap between them.

Hardy and I were chatting up a storm. He poured me a glass. He refilled his own glass. And so we went, very comfortably enjoying our starter. When the waiter came to clear our plates, the woman next to me said to him, 'Please ask the tourists next to me to stop drinking our wine?'

Before the waiter could open his mouth, I turned to the woman, with whom I was practically shoulder to shoulder, and said, 'Je suis désolé, madame!' (I'm so sorry, madam!)

I could smell her perfume, and noticed the gold specks in her grass-green eyes. Before I could say anything more, she said, in perfect English, with only the faintest trace of a French accent, 'You may pour me a glass of your wine. I can see that you have exceptional taste.'

We'd ordered the very same Burgundy wine from Château de Meursault. Their bottle was just a better vintage.

We became new best friends right there. We even went with them to their apartment on one of the Grands Boulevards near the Palais Garnier. They have a fantastic art collection – a Rodin sculpture of a Greek youth stands beside a striding Giacometti man. There's a Renoir, too, and a Degas pastel sketch. Hopefully, in the near future there'll also be a LJvV. So, dear reader, not all Froggies are frogs.

But back to Gilles, whose irritated hand was gesturing for us to slide in next to Shrek and his wife. Remember, the rest of the dining area is completely empty. 'No,' I say to Gilles, who casually moves the woman's bag to the floor, 'S'il vous plait, laissez-nous nous asseoir là?' (Please let us sit there?) My voice almost hits a high F as I point to the empty tables all around.

He does not even deign to look at me. 'Non! Asseyez-vous ici' (No! Sit here). Gilles moves the chair next to Shrek like it's a matador's red cloak.

'No,' I say, livid, in French, 'the room is empty. I don't want to sit on top of anyone. I want to sit at that table.'

'No,' says Gilles. 'No. All of those tables are reserved.'

'All of them?' I ask.

'Certainement, oui!' He stands back from the chair he has pulled out for me; like a traffic officer, he starts trying to wave me into my parking spot.

Shrek and his wife chew loudly on their duck bones, oblivious to the fuss. My ears start to ring, and I recall the friendly, well-informed waiters at Yotam Ottolenghi's Nopi, in London.

'Fuck off, Gilles. You're a Spanish cow,' I bark, waving my hand extravagantly in front of his face and then up into the air. I realise I've mixed my metaphors again, but it works perfectly in this situation. In the process, I whack a water glass by accident – it shatters a good few tables away. At this dramatic moment I turn on my heel and storm out.

The manageress starts with a question at the door, but I throw my hands up into the air and huff like a Frenchman. That's the end of it!

As the Welsh actor and composer Ivor Novello said in 1941, 'There's something Vichy about the French.'

Before this incident, we'd often take our La Creuzette guests to this bistro when Paris was on the itinerary. We'd usually strike it lucky, and end up with one of the friendly waiters.

As you can imagine, it's not an easy task when Hardy and I have to translate the entire menu for the hungry guests. This one turns her nose up at the rabbit, that one can't stop laughing about the frog's legs in white sauce.

When we're less lucky, Gilles struts around our table, his ankle-length apron impeccably clean, its linen serviette hung neatly in the belt, his thin lips pulled into a peevish half-moon. When he leans forward in his patent leather shoes, you catch a whiff of something soapy but dusty at the same time.

One night, we're sitting with a bunch of demonstrative South Africans in the bistro, Gilles pacing around us. After dispensing with the starter and main course, with a great deal of effort and grumbling, he stands before us with the dessert menu. He casts his eyes towards the ceiling, like a snail, as if looking for flies.

One of our guests – Fluitjie Viljoen, a bulky lady with three or four French lessons under her belt, sighs with shiny, buttery lips in Gilles's direction: 'Je suis plein.'

From his lofty height he looks down at her for a moment, then says, with a sneer, 'Cela est évident, madame' (That much is clear, madam). He clasps his hands piously in front of his chest, as if he's

153

Our first group of guests with chef Marlene van der Westhuizen (fourth from left).

Bread is the best!

Hardy and I with Anet Pienaar-Vosloo in front of
the famous Lapérouse restaurant in Paris.

just uttered a biblical truth. Fluitjie had translated the word 'full' directly into French as 'plein'. She meant to say that her appetite was satisfied, but what actually came out was 'I am pregnant.'

'Pregnant' Fluitjie's companion, Lientjie Louw, is a sensitive woman. She's already asked us to turn off the air conditioning in the bus, as she is susceptible to draughts. I hear one of the other guests grumble, 'That's because you're always so draughtily clad.' *Come on, guys, that's not nice*, I think.

Our table is across the way from an open door and window. Lientjie is bothered by the light breeze that's keeping us all cool-headed. For the hundredth time, she says she could catch her death from a draught. It's hot inside the bistro, but she won't hear of going to sit outside on the terrace: that could be the last straw.

She's clearly also been to classes at the Alliance Française in Cape Town, with her friend. She says bravely to Gilles, 'Ferme la porte, je suis froid.' She meant that she was getting cold, which was why she wanted Gilles to close the door, but by saying 'je suis froid' she actually said that she was frigid. In France, you never say 'I am hot' or 'I am cold.' This has a sexual meaning. Instead, you say, 'J'ai chaud,' or 'I have heat.' You can get yourself into big trouble by talking about the other way of getting warm.

Oblivious to this, Lientjie glares at Gilles as he puts a large slice of strawberry tart down in front of her. The crème de marron drips over the edge of her bowl; she licks the syrupy sauce off her fingers with relish. Biiiig mistake!

Giles pulls a face of pure shock and takes a step back, his hands two stop signs in front of his chest. 'Laissez tomber, madame!' (Leave that, madam!)

Quelle horreur!

156

French wine stewards are in a different class, mercifully. The better restaurants have a sommelier or wine master on hand to help you with your choice.

In Montluçon, we befriend a generous sommelier who teaches us the finer points of French wine etiquette. His name is extraordinarily apt: Philip d'Canter, which sounds like 'decanter'. Imagine that! Monsieur d'Canter has a sharp sense of humour. He tells us that you always need to let a good bottle of red wine breathe, but that if you can no longer hear it breathing after a while, mouth-to-mouth is the only option. Cheers, my friend!

The French often tell the following joke: how do you spot a tourist or newcomer? It's the person drinking red wine on its own. French people don't usually drink red wine without a meal.

Of course, there is a multitude of other drinks that *can* be drunk on their own. Champagne is high on the list. I still think it's stylish to serve a good champagne when your guests arrive, and to serve it again with the dessert. It also looks lovely when the glasses stand in a row above each plate: first the water glass, then the white wine and red wine glasses, and then the champagne glass.

When you drink in France, bread is never far away. Bread is part of the French national consciousness. I will never forget the observation written on a little wooden board outside a village bistro: 'Bread is the warmest, kindest of all words. Always write it with a capital letter, like your name.'

A French menu is unthinkable without bread, which plays the lead role. The baguette, with its crispy golden crust, is especially important. The French are very precious about their bread. The baguette has to be just right, or there'll be trouble. The ideal baguette is about 70 cm long and weighs between 150 and 175 g. In the dining room at home, or at the restaurant, the bread is the first to come to the table. It remains an important part of the meal up to and including the cheese, which is usually the fourth dish.

The croissant is originally from Austria, but the French adopted it without scruples. Breakfast in France – and at La Creuzette – is inconceivable without one. Hardy usually bakes a dozen or so for our guests early each morning. The pain au chocolat and Parisienne are two delicious progeny of the humble croissant.

There must be at least half a dozen other classic types of bread available, the couronne and the ficelle being firm favourites. With the new trend towards gluten-free baking and the rediscovery of old types of flour that are not necessarily wheat-based, scores of variations on the old theme are emerging. Buckwheat is the new black, yells the young baker on the market square. It's overwhelming: now, I'm learning about millet bread and pea flour, not to mention almond and coconut bread!

When all's been said about bread and wine in France, water is next – as it says somewhere in the book of Matthew, man shall not live by bread alone. We all know the famous bottled waters – Evian, Volvic and Perrier – but there is one brand that towers head and shoulders over all others. You will impress the French beyond measure if you serve them their best-kept secret: Chateldon. This is a rare mineral water that is naturally bubbly. It comes from the heart of the Puy de Dôme region, which has dozens of springs. Since the time of Louis XIV and Louis XV, Chateldon has been known for its health-giving properties. The king's doctors recommended it to everyone who would listen – and who could afford it.

Since then, the bottles have appeared on the tables of most leading restaurants.

When we encounter this sparkling water for the first time, Hardy and I are sitting in a la-di-da rooftop restaurant overlooking the shimmering city of Paris. The Eiffel Tower shivers and glints like a crystal rocket on the brink of firing off into the universe.

When we hesitate a bit to pay the fairly high price for a bottle of Chateldon, the wasp-bodied waiter raises his eyebrows to just this side of the skylights in the roof. 'Rip-off – I'm just having a glass of tap water,' Hardy still hisses through his teeth. Which is exactly what the snipe of a waiter proposes: 'Perhaps you should try the Château Robinet or Château la Pompe.' Tap water or pump water.

Since that day's crippling defeat, I've taken to yelling, 'Chateldon, s'il vous plaît!' right at the restaurant's front door.

'As only you could,' my father would say, his dark eyebrows rumpled into an impatient frown.

# 14

## A house filled with love

During the renovation of La Creuzette – or, rather, its complete recreation – we live for a few months like moles beneath the dust. The *taupe*, or mole, is an industrious worker, but, as anyone who owns a lawn will attest, he is blind.

When we finally have the chance to catch our breath one Saturday morning, it coincides with the day of the duchess's first visit since she sold us our little palace. We spit and polish as is fitting. Hardy conjures up a massive wildflower arrangement in the entrance hall. The chipped Baccarat vase we bought at last Sunday's brocante in the next village shines like the morning star. The crack on the rim of the beautiful pot is turned to the back; the pot is on the piano that we bought from the family.

Apparently, Chopin played some of his very last études on this instrument. No, really, it's true. One of our neighbouring villages is Nohant, where George Sand lived with Frédéric Chopin for a good while in her château. As I've mentioned, Sand visited Boussac often. She even wrote one of her books here. She was friends with our duchess's forefathers, and sold them the piano in our entrance hall.

The duchess comes for tea and we serve elegant slices of plum tart with whipped cream. She eats hers delicately, her cake fork polished to a shine. The room smells of perfume and cinnamon.

'It's a house of love, this . . . please, sirs, keep it so,' she says suddenly. The light plays in her blue eyes as she looks through the wide windows at the huge beech tree in the middle of the garden – a giant leaf umbrella from which the barn owl calls through our nights.

'When I was ten years old, I would play with my doll Janine under the majestic tree. It's my favourite place in all the world.' She shifts forwards a little in her chair.

'One day, a car drove through the gates and drew to a halt at La Creuzette's imposing stairs. I watched everyone, with my doll on my lap. Two adults got out, and opened the back door. A little boy with pitch-black hair got out. He wore a suit with a blood-red tie,' she continues. 'The adults gestured towards me, where I sat under the tree. He walked across the lawn, right up to me. He extended a hand to me, formally, and said, in the loveliest voice I'd ever heard, "Bonjour, mademoiselle, je m'appelle Renaud Saint Gal de Pons." I knew instantly that he was my knight in shining armour.'

She smiles, and takes a sip of coffee. 'We married on 30 August 1934, and this house has been filled with love ever since.'

The duke and duchess were blessed with seven children and, later, a wealth of grandchildren and great-grandchildren. The decades passed; life played out beautifully at La Creuzette.

Needless to say, we take the duchess's request to heart; we want to keep the flame of La Creuzette's love alight. We suspect we've got it right: in the time we've lived in this place of wondrous beauty, exquisite stories of our own have played themselves out too.

Take the formidable woman from the south, well into her seventies, and the diamond dealer from northern Europe, who came to paint with me. The spark between them was instant – a petit frisson, as the French say. Seeing these two creative people fall in love – at first timid and shy, later frisky and sportive – was too beautiful for words. And, speaking of sports, they would leave, later, in his soft-top sports car for Tuscany, where he owned a farmhouse.

It's a sight I will never forget – his cap dapper on his head, her Hermès scarf elegant, holding her still-dark curls in place. They roar away in a cloud of smoke, the radio tuned to Chérie FM, Nolwenn Leroy singing, 'Juste pour me souvenir ...'

But the story that is, to me, most emblematic of La Creuzette's romanticism and enchantment unfolds like this. Throughout the year, students come to La Creuzette to help out with the many different tasks that form part of the château's daily routine. If you're familiar with the complex machinery of hotels, restaurants and guesthouses, you'll know that you need to take things by the horns for it all to run smoothly – especially when there are high standards to uphold.

The students come from near and far – America, England, France, Austria and Canada. But most of them come from South Africa. The internships started as a favour that we wanted to do for our women friends with daughters (and sons). They've become so popular that there's now a long waiting list.

One year, as part of the prize, the whole *Kokkedoor* team came for the semi-final to shoot an episode at La Creuzette. What a carnival that was! *Kwêla* presenter Therese Benade, who reported on the *Kokkedoor* shoot, and I chattered away like old friends. She told me that she knew a very dear person whom she thought would be perfect for the internship. This person was unlike anyone else, she promised us.

The blue-eyed DeVerra Auret arrives in France with the spring blossoms – after her father exhorts her not to go and just fall in love with any old Frenchman. 'Dad, I listen to my head, not just to my heart,' she answers.

As the VLV ladies would say, DeVerra is one to grab things with both hands. Over and above the energetic way in which she carries out her tasks, she is a designer to boot, who can also attend to the aesthetic side of things. This earns her a double plus in my little blue book.

Between the season's summer tours, there are always a few days of free time for the young interns to relax and catch their breath before the next tour. On one such occasion, there is a music concert in the school hall. Everything that breathes is there – everything under 30, that is. The sociable DeVerra and another intern befriend a group of nice young people; they all go back to someone's house to party after the concert.

It's a festive affair and the lovely DeVerra soon has a youngster vying for her affection. Cellphone in sweaty hand, he Google Translates their way through a conversation. Soon, a friend comes along and introduces a young man *en passant* (in passing) to their group. DeVerra's heart misses a beat. Not only is the Frenchman very attractive, but he speaks English too. Monsieur Google Translate notices the flush on DeVerra's cheeks when she meets this Antonin. He intensifies his cyber-translation strategy, shifts possessively closer to her and bombards the poor girl with fiery requests.

The Duke and Duchess of St Gal de Pons
on their wedding day at La Creuzette.

Therese Benade interviews me for the TV programme *Kwêla*.

DeVerra Auret (left), manager of La Creuzette, and Maya Grey ready to welcome guests to one of our receptions.

I'm convinced that Aphrodite is responsible for the fact that Antonin joins their group a second time. At that moment, Google Translate's insistence becomes too much for DeVerra.

'Please help me,' she says, flustered, looking Antonin right in the eyes.

She tells me later that it felt like an eternity before Antonin declared, 'Let go of her arm. I am taking her home.' He takes a step closer to the overenthusiastic youngster.

DeVerra says her polite goodbyes and thank yous to everyone in the group and walks away with Antonin without so much as a backward glance. By now, Monsieur Google Translate's batteries are flat. As the French say, *les carottes sont cuites* (the carrots are cooked, meaning it's too late).

But this lovely episode happens just before the students' summer term at La Creuzette ends. DeVerra is heartbroken that she has to go back to South Africa. There and then, Hardy, DeVerra and I decide that La Creuzette needs a manager; we two men could do with another set of accomplished hands.

To be quite sure that the Frenchman is worth our trouble, however, we decide to hold an impromptu interview with the unsuspecting fellow. To get the measure of him, as the old people would say.

I decide to award him points in my head. It's not long before he's scored a healthy eight – after he tells me which books he reads, among other things. James Joyce, *nogal*.

Antonin is a nature lover. A few weeks earlier, when he came courting, I told him about an interesting 19th-century painting technique. It was fashionable, then, for artists to use a tiny feather that grows on the edge of the woodcock's wing to paint water-colours. The painting would also usually depict the bird itself in its natural habitat. It's a time-consuming process, and you really have to know what you're doing to work with such a delicate brush. The feather would be clasped in a special silver-and-ebony holder. The two together look like an old-fashioned pen and nib. The feather and, sometimes, the whole holder would then be framed with the watercolour.

I tell Antonin that I find these kinds of peculiarities of artistic taste very interesting, and that, one day, I would like to try this particular one. The problem is, where do you even start looking for a woodcock feather?

When our interview concludes that day, Antonin scores a nine.

On his departure, he takes a small envelope out of his shirt pocket. 'Woodcock feathers for your aquarelle,' he says, smiling broadly.

I can hardly believe my eyes. *This* is what I call a ten-out-of-ten person.

'As God is my witness, DeVerra, if you do not take this man, I will!' I exclaim.

We laugh ourselves to tears.

# 15

# Wedding fever

In France, weddings take on an entirely different shape. They are nothing like South African celebrations. The event usually spans three days: first, the civil ceremony in the town hall on a Friday evening, followed by a family dinner in a local hotel; then the church wedding on the Saturday, with a reception; and then a luncheon, on the Sunday, for close family only. Only then does the couple depart for *la lune de miel* or *voyage de noce* – the honeymoon.

These days, the youngsters are in a hurry and use only the Saturday and the Sunday. On the Saturday morning, the mayor concludes the official wedding in the town hall. Then, the wedding party simply walks over to the stone church in their full regalia; it's usually just around the corner from the mairie. The enfants d'honneur lead the procession; there is no such thing as a flower girl or pageboy in France.

After the church service, the guests go to the *vin d'honneur*, a large reception that is usually held in a park or in the *salle des fêtes* (village hall). It's a big affair; many people are invited. There is mostly just standing room, although a few chairs and benches are set out for the older guests. The party often starts at five in the afternoon, so that by about eight in the evening it's over – and the bridal couple and a smaller group of family and friends can move to the *repas de noce* (wedding dinner).

The younger guard may have only one function, which carries on until at least five the following morning. It's here that the lovely tradition of serving the guests a bowl of steaming onion soup, as the clock strikes five, is upheld. This is the signal for Ferreira to take his *goed* and *trek*. The gift for the guests is usually a little bag or box containing five candied almonds – *la boîte à dragées*.

Choosing a wedding cake is a serious business, just as important as the bride's dress and the wedding march. It's no laughing matter, my Auntie Polly would say with a sigh, popping a little white icing-sugar dove into her mouth. Why do people always eat wedding-cake decorations? Isn't it supposed to be all about the rich, cognac-soaked fruitcake underneath the whole marzipan story?

The minute the bridal couple pull the door of the wedding car shut, the guests descend like locusts on the cake. I've seen, with my very own eyes, a woman licking the base of the little plastic bride and groom figures clean before stuffing them into her faux ostrich leather handbag. Together with two wine glasses. I nearly fell out of my chair once at a Brakpan wedding when the wedding cake was rolled into the hall, with great ceremony, on a trolley. The entire cake was made of koeksisters, half-dipped in chocolate. If I remember correctly, the trolley made its entrance to the strains of Sonja Herholdt's 'Jantjie kom huis toe'. The guests started a spontaneous foot-stamping; the cake made the front page of the *Brakpan Herald*.

The classic fruitcake remains, well, the classic wedding option. I remember a terribly modern version of a wedding cake being brought before us in Middelburg once. Weeks after the glamorous wedding, people were still enthusing over the phenomenon. The baker made the bottom layer of the cake out of cardboard, and put a secret little door in it. Inside this layer were small bars of fruit-cake. Each had a line of marzipan icing sugar on top, and was wrapped in see-through cellophane – the kind that makes those high-pitched mouse noises when you try to remove it. Believe me, sitting in a hall and hearing 300 pieces of cellophane squeaking at the same time is a deeply irritating experience.

La Creuzette has seen scores of weddings in her day, from the duchess's own wedding, on 13 August 1934, to those of her seven children and, later, her grandchildren. The oldest grandchild drew the shortest straw: by that time, the duchess was no longer around and the family wealth had eroded substantially. As the story goes, the family had a meeting and decided to fell one of the oldest oak trees on the grounds and saw it up to sell as wood for furniture. Blue-blooded Frenchmen don't take out bank loans! The flashy wedding could proceed after that.

To this day, we host weddings frequently at La Creuzette: the grounds are exceptionally well-suited for this. We once hosted a wedding celebration, complete with all the accompanying bells and whistles, for a Namibian couple. Since people of the desert seem to like escaping from the heat, they picked a date in October. The time of spontaneous cloudbursts in our region, unfortunately.

The guests sit, silent and stately, around the seven tables under the cedar trees. The candles flicker. The couple married before the magistrate a week ago. The DJ tries to play the bride and bridegroom's favourite song for the third time, but every time they emerge from the château's entrance hall it starts to rain.

Kaboom! A thunderclap sounds from the grey heavens, rattling the chandeliers. Then everything goes dark. The poor bride has to stay on the bridegroom's arm until, in pitch blackness, we can flick the main switch in the cellar back to 'on'. Eventually, the DJ gets the music going again and the two walk out to Rihanna's 'Stay'.

They are halfway down the red carpet when the heavens open and the rain falls with an unprecedented urgency. As unexpectedly as it started, it stops, and the sun's last rays stream cheerfully through the clouds. Everyone laughs in relief and shifts on their damp cushions. The bride's flame-red ostrich feather boa has seen better days, but her mascara, according to the maid of honour, is waterproof, luckily. Her unyielding curls have been so thoroughly lacquered that it's going to take more than a few raindrops to ruin that festive hairdo.

The master of ceremonies, a real comedian, assures the guests that it takes more than a bit of rain to scare off a Namibian. To the contrary, the Nama regard it as good luck if it rains during a wedding ceremony. The couple's path will be strewn with desert roses, he says.

The family has hauled the four layers of fruitcake for the wedding cake all the way from Namibia – along with half a dozen bottles of date brandy from the Okahandja district. It becomes a merry party.

Early the next morning, the bride's aunt asks Martine, the housekeeper, whether she can use the microwave in the bedroom wardrobe to heat up her milk for the Ricoffy she's brought with her.

'No, madame, that will not work. That is a safe for your earrings and cash, and certainly not for warming milk,' Martine answers, put out. We all agree that the lady's mistaking the safe for a microwave is the fault of the date brandy.

The traditional French wedding cake is the much-loved croquembouche. Like the Tuscan villa, this spectacular tower is very popular in South Africa these days. It was designed in the late 1700s by Antonin Carême as part of his series of pièce-montée desserts to grace the table as sculpture. The name originates from 'croque' and 'bouche' – a crunch in the mouth. A mouth-cruncher!

At our request, once, the baker in the village designs a croquembouche for a difficult couple who are celebrating their 50th wedding anniversary. After champagne and croquembouche have been served in the gardens of La Creuzette, everyone will move to the hotel for the dinner.

From the outset, Agnès locks horns with the baker. She can't decide on the filling for the profiteroles – it's almond cream, then it's rose cream, then it's chocolate ganache. She's also not satisfied with the height of the tower; Cyril, her perennially smiling husband, has to measure her height when she is seated at the table so that the pyramid will be exactly 15 cm taller than her.

Agnès also wants their initials to be worked in, here and there, between the balls of the croquembouche. On the big night, two French waiters bring the cake to the main table at the appointed time. The impressive croquembouche is covered in shades of golden caramel, with their initials, 'CA CA', written everywhere, in almond cream, between the balls. The French pronounce the letter 'c' as a hard 'k' when it precedes certain vowels. So, if you read this in Afrikaans ...

I have to say, it was very hard not to burst out laughing. Luckily, I could contain myself and propose a toast to the slightly tipsy, blushing couple.


Speaking of weddings, it's a miserable day in early March 2013 when Hardy asks if he could see me in the office. He wants to have a little talk. The office is in the fourth-floor attic; it's a long climb to get there.

Whenever he wants to talk formally like this, it's usually about finances – in most cases, it's because I've bought something for the house without his permission. Again. When I've caught my breath after the ascent, it appears I'm not that far off: this does have something vaguely to do with finances.

'We need to get married,' he says, without flinching.

He looks a bit uncomfortable and continues. The accountant has suggested that we get married to make the tax system work in our favour. He starts babbling, quoting percentages and amounts as if he's lecturing a group of BCom students.

'No,' I say. 'Not so fast. Give me a day or so to process this.'

I start the long hike back downstairs. 'Stop playing hard to get, now. The accountant reckons the sooner the better,' he mumbles after me.

That night, in front of the TV, just before we start watching a new series of *Game of Thrones*, I say, smarting, 'It's not like I expected you to go down on one knee to pop the question, but still. So cool and calculated. Not very stylish, is it?'

'What's with you now?' Hardy asks through a mouthful of pop-corn.

'Look,' I say, taking the remote out of his hand and pressing pause. I don't stand a chance if it's the Lannisters I have to compete with for attention. 'Here's the deal.' I'm full of daring. 'We're going to Paris on Wednesday. We can have a look at Cartier at those Russian wedding bands I like so much.'

I press play. Just before the prince chops off the head of an unsuspecting nobleman, Hardy says, 'Okay, then.'

And that's that.

The civil ceremony takes place at 5 pm on a Tuesday afternoon at the mairie on Boussac's town square. Needless to say, in Paris I visited not only Cartier but also Christian Lacroix; my good suit has seen better days – and, really, we're in *France*.

There's a photographer, and there's Françoise and her husband, Claude, as witnesses. That's all. It's later that evening that the grandest feast will happen at La Creuzette. Our beloved mayor is decked out in the official regalia of the République française. I shudder every time I set eyes on that impressive ceinture in the French colours. The gold tassels where the two ends of the sash come together look just like ringing bells.

Ours is the first same-sex marriage to take place in our village – indeed, in the whole region. We can see how nervous the mayor is. When we eventually take our seats on the two baroque gold chairs in front of his desk, he stands and holds one hand up in the air.

'Today, we make history – not only in our village, but in all of Limousin. I have decided that, instead of delivering the abbreviated version of the official wedding formulary, I will deliver the full version. But, before I begin, I wish to break with tradition to tell you two new Frenchmen that, today, I speak not only for myself when I deliver a message on behalf of the whole village.'

It feels like my heart's in a vice.

'We all have the greatest respect and appreciation for you both, and wish to assure you that we regard you as an important part of our community. Here, you are loved.'

He looks at us and smiles a tooth-bearing smile. The lump in my throat becomes two tears that fall onto my brand-new jacket. Unseen, mercifully.

I can't help comparing it to our first wedding, six years earlier, in the Boland. (The French did not legally acknowledge our South African wedding and that is why we had to get married there again.) Ton and Anet were our witnesses. It was just the four of us – no fanfare. A song and dance was the last thing we wanted. It was the mid-1990s, shortly after the new Constitution made provision for such unions. Certain officials were still throwing their toys out of the cot, summarily refusing to join two men in matrimony.

Nonetheless, there we were, outside Malmesbury's municipal offices at the crack of dawn. When the man at the counter sees who the wedding couple is, he goes to call the official who will be performing the ceremony. It's a good while before he comes back, but when he does reappear, he says that Mr So-and-so will be ready in a minute. He's just getting the paperwork in order.

Twenty minutes later, there is no sign of him. My collar is getting scratchy. The carnation in Hardy's button hole is in dire need of water.

The official goes to enquire again, and shuffles back to us a short while later, deflated. The official is not available, he says.

'What do you mean? He was busy with the paperwork just a few minutes ago,' I say, leaning over the counter to try to understand,

'He has left,' the youngster says, embarrassed.

'How is that possible? He was right there in the office!' Hardy's voice climbs an octave or two.

'He climbed out the window.' The fellow's face is now as red as a beetroot.

'You cannot be serious!' I can hardly believe my ears.

'I'm sorry, sirs, but that's God's own truth. Mr So-and-so is the only official who has the authority to solemnise a marriage.'

'It's a sign,' I say to Anet, who slides in behind the wheel. 'Let's just leave it. What does it matter anyway?'

'For what?' says Ton. 'We're going to Paarl.'

Anet calls ahead and they give her the green light. And so we race through the wheatfields of the Swartland, in full song: 'Pollie, ons gaan Pêrel toe, Pollie, ons gaan Pêrel toe.'

Ms Matthews receives us in a hot, muggy building in Paarl. Her good-natured, open face puts us at ease; I can finally stop shaking. Anet fixes Hardy's limp carnation so that it stands tall once again.

'We are aware of what happened to you at Malmesbury. Before I begin, I just want to tell you two brave men that this will be a first for me, too, but that I perform this duty with pride. I know how it feels to be regarded as a second-class citizen. My people have also struggled.' When she looks me straight in the eye and smiles, a lump pushes up in my throat.

When Ms Matthews comes to the part when she asks whether you take so-and-so as your lawfully wedded husband, she uses my name for both parties by mistake. If Ton hadn't said something, I'd have married myself. We all have a good laugh. The ice is broken, the lump in my throat subsides, and our carnations stand bolt upright in our buttonholes.

One can't help comparing our elegant French wedding with the Malmesbury fiasco and the encounter in the Pêrel of the Cape to which it would lead. What will stay with me for all my days remaining, however, is not necessarily the pomp in France, but the depth of the humanity that Ms Matthews displayed when she tied the knot for us that day.

*Right above and below:*
Hardy and I get
married at the
Home Affairs office
in Paarl, with the
friendly Ms Matthews
in the middle.

*Below and opposite:*
Our wedding day in
France, with the
mayor of Boussac,
Franck Foulon (centre),
and our friends
Claude and Françoise.

# 16

## Laughing myself fluent – in French

Ouma Bettie, my fierce granny, would always say that a good cry comes of a good laugh. She had so many sayings that we found amusing as children. And when we'd start laughing, nothing but a good hiding could get us to keep quiet.

My sister, whose nickname was Katrous, would laugh so hard that she'd wet her pants, which would send us all into hysterics. My father was known for dishing out hidings to foolish children. I'd receive the first hiding, for wanting to see the wet pants. My father's hidings were always backhanders: if he was to hit us with his palm, he'd send us all the way into tomorrow. Another of Ouma Bettie's priceless sayings.

I can't remember ever laughing as much as I used to in those days with Ouma Bettie. Well, not until I came to live in the French countryside, that is. Now, we laugh ourselves silly at the strange sayings that Asterix's *mense* use.

When someone in France faints, or starts feeling faint, they say with a deep sigh, 'Elle tombe dans les pommes' (She's falling among the apples). Not into a bed of roses, or onto a Chanel No 5-scented blanket. Nope. Among the apples. It may sound quite poetic the first time you hear it, but on reflection it's a bit odd, not so?

If you're not interested in Brigitte or Jean-Claude's romantic overtures and you don't want to go out with them, you give them the rake. That's right, the expression *se prendre un râteau* (to step on a rake) means to be turned down. I've heard of giving someone a dressing down, but a rake? Well, I never.

When the French want to indicate that something is easy – 'easy as pie', as we say in English – they say they do it 'les doigts dans le nez' (with fingers in the nose). The expression was originally used when a horse had a convincing lead in a race. How weird is that?

When we first got to France, we would often have to go to great lengths to avoid offending our new countrymen. A good laugh, in any event, is *inconvenant*, according to the French etiquette books – properly improper.

The French are generally friendly and helpful if you manage to tread the water of their lovely language. Of course, there are many exceptions to this rule. Even when we'd been living in France for a good few years, I'd still run into many a French frog. Take, for example, the day I want to thank the bus driver when I get off the bus at the Louvre in Paris. I try my level best to make my 'merci beaucoup' sound as melodious as possible, but what slips out of my sloppy lips sounds more like 'merci beau-cul, monsieur' (Thank you nice ass, sir). He glares at me, eyes afire. The bus door opens with an almighty hiss. 'Bof!' he croaks, so animatedly that his cap slips down over his eyes.

I give a feeble wave, but the bus pulls away before my feet have found solid ground. I land on all fours in front of a group of Japanese tourists, ambling along behind a tour guide with a yellow umbrella. One of them actually tosses a two-euro coin in front of me. My dignity is in tatters.

One of the most common blunders is in the difference between how the 'ou' and 'u' sounds are pronounced in French. 'Dessous' is pronounced 'desoo', and 'dessus' is pronounced 'desie'. One means 'under', the other 'on top'.

I'd rather not go into detail about how this particular business landed me in hot water once. I will leave a clue, however, that comes from an old Afrikaans folk song: *'Dis jou kombers en my matras, en daar lê die ding.'*

One day, a French television channel sends an outspoken Parisienne to interview us about our comings and goings in the French countryside. In our area, there are literally a few hundred old castles lying forgotten, waiting for people like us – people who are crazy enough to take them on. Local residents and the government try hard to talk people into restoring the area's historical buildings. They even offer a subsidy to inspire people to take up their trowels. The municipality of Boussac offered us such a subsidy, but it was tiny. A condition of accepting it was also that we would be obliged to open the house to the public. We politely declined.

Madame Listen-here from the television channel wears a skew little trilby that rattles the dogs the first time we meet her. While the cameraman is setting up his impressive lenses, Madame tells us how and what and where she wants us to perform. To me, she comes across as abrupt and stern. Hardy finds her charming!

It doesn't help that she doesn't like the painting of mine that's hanging in the entrance hall. She has her assistant replace it with a pallid tapestry. She chatters away to Hardy about absolutely everything. We keep having to chase our two dogs away: Madame is apparently scared of large hunting dogs.

My turn in front of the cameras comes around. They are shooting the scene in front of the house, under the wild chestnut trees. Cameras rolling, I become Cary Grant under the trees, which are in blossom. One of the dogs walks past, in front of the camera. We have to start again. I launch into my piece as if it's Oscar night.

My moment of glory is short-lived. 'Cut!' Madame shouts, for the hundredth time. By this time my cheeks are flushed and I have dark sweat stains under my arms. The assistant's powdering doesn't do very much. My face is a light bulb, but I persevere.

'Ta gueule,' Madame shrieks.

In any language, dear reader, this translates as a rude 'Shut up.'

'Vous parlez français comme une vache espagnole,' she barks.

Evidently I speak French like a Spanish cow. Exit Cary Grant.

She is most satisfied to have Hardy in my place in front of the cameras, and does a showy little dance when he gets the job done in just one take. It's a dance, however, that excites one of the dogs. She storms this woman she does not know. Madame's screams inflame her even more and she promptly bites Madame on the calf.

The commotion that follows is indescribable. Madame tugs her Hermès belt open and pulls her white studded trousers down to her ankles. The dog's canine has thankfully not pierced the flesh; it's left only a red mark.

She calls her doctor in Paris who assures her that, in spite of it all, she will live. Madame demands the dog's papers from Hardy so that she can be sure she has not contracted rabies. She gives me dirty looks for the rest of the day. As if I incited the dog to attack her. Perhaps dogs can read minds after all, and the poor dog was simply defending her owner.

Hardy and I have a good laugh once the team has left. I laugh loudest at the hideous Bridget Jones pantaloons we all had to behold when Madame pulled down her trousers. Definitely not what you'd expect from a chic French lady.

I go and find the dog in the garden, and give her a hug and an extra-thick slice of fillet. Spanish cow. Can you believe it?

It takes many years and many tears and much laughter for one's Frenchness to start kicking in. Ours was a slow and eventful transformation, much of which happened while we were eating: everything from frog's legs – yes, really – to the most feared sausage on earth: the bloody andouillette.

The andouillette is another animal altogether. It's a coarsely ground affair, made of offal from various sources, mixed with pork of some description. Which could well be the head and the tail. It's a stout little sausage: seven or eight centimetres long and about three centimetres across.

The bugger has a tremendously bad aroma. It smells like something you've trodden in by accident in the farmyard. It's usually concealed in an onion-and-wine sauce that makes most people head for the hills. Can you believe that the French even thread this stinking sausage onto a sosatie stick?

Françoise, my best French friend and confidante, always invites us for one last meal before we go back to South Africa on holiday. She sets the table with her special Limoges porcelain and the family's silver cutlery. There are always a few good bottles of Bordeaux breathing on the sideboard.

When she invited us the first time, she told us that she'd be making an original Creusoise coq au vin. With thoughts of a tasty Nando's bird, I sit, my mouth watering, at Françoise's lovely table on the appointed evening.

She serves a delicious Jerusalem artichoke soup as a starter.

'It's quite a thing to prepare the traditional coq au vin,' she says, wiping her mouth with her serviette. 'I bought the chicken from the farmer myself, and had to take the housekeeper with me so that she could whisk the fresh chicken blood in a jug to stop it from clotting. You need it to make the trademark wine sauce.'

She takes another sip of wine, and starts collecting our soup bowls. I drain my glass and take a stealthy sip from Hardy's. The chicken-slaughtering, blood-whisking scene plays out in my mind's eye. I don't hear another word that the host and the other guests are saying. All I can see is the woman in the passenger seat, fork in hand. Whisk, whisk, whisk. The sound of the fork in the enamel jug is upsetting enough.

The plates are set down before us. Each reveals a dark piece of chicken, a few slices of Vitelotte potato, and a serving of grass-green peas. Françoise comes around with a jug of sauce, deftly pouring a syrupy waterfall of pitch-black sauce over the chicken. Her movements are in slow-mo.

Fortunately, the host has filled our glasses. At the outset I take a large sip from Hardy's glass: I know I'm going to need my full quota to get myself out of this predicament. I wish the sideboard was on my side; if it were, I could get stuck into the bottle myself.

The sauce has a unique taste, which the expert chef would say has a high umami score. To me, it tastes like liquid iron, not unlike

Hardy impresses the television crew from
Paris with his excellent French.

I, on the other hand,
was asked to paint but not speak a word of French . . .

the taste of blood you get when you've just had a free hiding from the school bully. If it wasn't for the taste, you'd swear it was molasses.

My glass and my plate are empty before I utter the fatal words: 'This is my absolute favourite dish.' I make a show of licking my lips. My friend gives a broad smile and brings out the cheese board. She signals to Claude to pour more wine.

The year flies by. We're invited again for the annual farewell meal at Françoise's. She lets me know well in advance that she'll be preparing my favourite dish again – this time, with extra sauce. Especially for me. I try all my usual excuses, but not a single one works. The date has already changed three times.

Before we leave home, I knock a few back to reckon with the dreaded sauce in advance. When the main course comes, the jug of sauce is put on the Salton hot tray, right next to the bottles of wine. Quel calvaire! (What an ordeal!)

The nightmare sauce behind me, I clear my throat and come clean. 'Forgive my white lie, Françoise, but I don't actually like blood sauce. I much prefer your delicious vegetable pie. I've been a closet vegetarian since I was small, and am seriously considering doing the whole vegan thing.'

And so it is that, here in Boussac, I learn to stop embroidering on the truth. You know, that white lie you tell now to please someone, and that lands you in hot water down the line.

From that day forward, I never fib again. I've learnt my lesson, in the bloodiest of ways.

# 17

# The scenic route

Hardy is the only person I know who talks back to the GPS.

'Are you mad?' he shouts, almost driving into the kerb. I cling grimly to my seat and squeeze my eyes shut.

'The woman is insane,' he says, unplugging the cable that gives her life. 'French hussy! From now on I'm going with my gut.'

And this, dear reader, means only one thing: we're taking a detour, thanks to Hardy's built-in 'take the scenic route' program. He makes an illegal U-turn.

I've tried hard to convince him that he can change the woman's tinny voice to that of a young guy who speaks Afrikaans. But no, this he will not do. He's even given the French GPS voice a nickname: Jeanne.

'After Jeanne Moreau?' I ask.

'No,' he says.

'Jeanne d'Arc?'

'No.'

'Then who, in heaven's name?'

'Jeanne Calment,' he says, turning his head 45 degrees to be able to read the road sign better.

'Who the hell is Jeanne Calment?'

'The oldest French woman who ever lived. She made it to 122 years and 164 days.'

'Voilà!' I shriek, and take a bite out of one of the delicious yellow-green apples from our region. 'That makes complete sense: your GPS is also 122 years old!'

Hardy flatly refuses to update his GPS. New offramps are built on the highways, and whole apartment blocks are flattened to make way for shopping centres. Streets are made longer, or shorter, or given unexpected traffic circles. No wonder a bridge that his beloved Jeanne referred to one day no longer exists. The bridge – or what's left of it – may still be there, but the road becomes a dead end. I've begged him how many times, and even got out of the car once at a traffic light in protest, but aikôna.

So begin our journeys of discovery, off the beaten track, in rural France. But before I launch into our experiences of our region's natural beauty, let me add that this part of the world was re-named on 1 January 2016. The Limousin region now falls within the Nouvelle-Aquitaine, the largest administrative region in France, comprising much of the southwest of the country. The region was created after three regions – Aquitaine, Limousin and Poitou-Charentes – were merged in 2014.

This is how we end up, one day, in Collonges-la-Rouge, a village in the department of the Corrèze that looks like it comes straight from a Jean de la Fontaine fable. The village dates back to the 15th and 16th centuries, and is built from the reddish sandstone of the area. The rich colour is a result of the high concentration of iron oxide in the local sandstone.

It is a fairyland that glows. Wherever you look you see spires and steeply pitched roofs and bridges arching over the river. I have never seen so many crooked vines together in one place. It feels as if the climbing vines and draping white and blue wisteria are taking over the farmhouses and imposing mansions, which stand shoulder to shoulder. Every wide stoep, every lane, is embraced by a soft, leafy dome.

There is a Kodak moment around every corner. I count at least 25 spires on the way to our restaurant. Luckily, I've brought my sketchbook. There and then, I plonk myself at the foot of a centuries-old vine, flat on my bum.

The meal on the cool stoep is also unforgettable. We have a well-known traditional dish from the region, a soup with the lovely name of 'bréjaude'. It's more of a potée than a soup, really, because it uses meat and vegetables in the same dish. Hardy's dish is a robust piece of pork rib with potatoes, turnips, carrots and shredded cabbage leaves, which swim in a clear, flavourful bouillon. I choose the vegetarian option. Splendide!

A mique – something between a bread and a dumpling – is served with the bréjaude. It's a taste capriole, out there on the shaded stoep.

What I also learn that day, on the side, is the history of the knife in France. I've never understood why there are no knives in the old sets of French silverware, only spoons and forks. Our friendly waiter explains that the French all used to own handmade pocket knives, which they'd carry with them wherever they went. When they got to the bistro, restaurant or local café, then, and ordered a tasty bréjaude, they'd eat the soup with the soup spoon that was laid out on the table. They'd simply cut their piece of pork, or whatever needed cutting, with their pocket knife. After the meal, they'd wipe the blade of their precious knife clean with the serviette, and fold it shut.

The handmade pocket knives of the Corrèze are world-famous. Stamped on the tempered steel blade is their characteristic symbol – a chestnut leaf.

The *chabrette* is another trademark of our region – a set of French bagpipes that's been played since the Middle Ages, at every occasion where more than three people have gathered. We're having our coffee when an old lady in traditional attire comes to stand in a corner of the stoep, her chabrette a giant cropper pigeon proudly pushing out its chest. When she's played her first few notes, a young man with a piano accordion steps up from another corner of the stoep to join her.

It is something truly special: the beauty of the high, wailing notes of the chabrette and the nostalgia of the piano accordion undo me. I want to burst into tears on the spot, but Hardy commands me to pull myself together. I can only imagine it's all the walnut liqueur I had with the clafoutis that's moved me so.

Speaking of liqueurs, allow me to sound a warning to all first-time visitors to France. It's about something that sounds like a very ugly word. But it's not the word that's ugly – it's the kick that hurts so much. Tread lightly around one of France's secret weapons: the pousse-café, a vicious one-for-the-road. Five different liqueurs, each a different colour, placed in one small glass before the unsuspecting guest.

The deceptive little rainbow in a glass kicks like a mule. If you're brave enough to have a second one, as the youngsters like to do, you'll start speaking *very* fluent French. Even after you've fallen asleep, the heartburn rips through you like wildfire.

Our scenic-route expeditions take us on idyllic meanders, far from the busy main roads and highways – experiences that make us forget all about the mêlée of the city.

It's all very calm and blissful – until you end up behind a VSP, or *voiture sans permis* (vehicle not requiring a licence). These little wheelbarrow cars have a top speed of 45 kph, and are banned from France's highways. Everyone and his uncle is allowed to buy one – from the *skollie* who's lost his driver's licence to the youngster who's not old enough yet to get one (anyone aged 14 and older may drive a VSP). On market days, strings of these little toy cars drive to the village. All you can do is wind down your window, and let the fresh air and the Chopin nocturnes on the CD player calm you down.

In 1982, the French government founded an association to identify the loveliest villages in France and support them financially. Les Plus Beaux Villages de France protects and advances the French *patrimoine*, which is a word that encompasses far more than its English translation (roughly, 'heritage'). It's not just a legacy that's entrusted to the individual. Rather, it's a sense of shared heritage, which is awarded to a community. Something that's passed, from the forefathers, from generation to generation. It comes from the Latin 'patrimonium', which literally means 'of the father'. Patrimoine is a concept that is very close to the French heart. For many people, it's their *raison d'être*.

Uzerche is a historic French village in the Corrèze. Like Boussac, it has existed since Roman times; a plaque declares proudly to visitors that the town has never been vanquished or occupied. It's no mean feat to have escaped the plundering of the French Revolution. The beautiful village is built in the crook of a dramatic

Walking in the footsteps of Vincent van Gogh
in Saint-Rémy-de-Provence.

At the gates of Saint-Paul de Mausole,
the mental hospital where Van Gogh received treatment,
which today houses a museum.

bend in the Vézère River. In 1787, the English author Arthur Young named Uzerche the pearl of the Limousin. And a pearl it is: the settlement is built on a steep rock formation, from which it watches like a prehistoric animal.

The Vézère is a tributary of the mighty, 211-kilometre-long Dordogne River. There is important prehistoric rock art, and artefacts, in caves along its banks.

It's here in Uzerche, in a tiny café with a creaking wooden stoep that hangs like a weaver's nest over the river, that we polish off our very first galétous in greedy bites. This is a buckwheat pancake that you enjoy either with Limousin honey or with grillons. I have to make the agonising choice between a galétous with miel mûrier du Limousin, which comes from blackberry blossoms, and rosemary honey, my other favourite.

When the waiter loses heart with me, Hardy orders pancakes with grillons. The waiter writes down his order with a blunt pencil. He asks again – rolling his eyes, this time – whether I've decided yet. Cheekily, I order both.

Grillons is a local pâté made with pork cubes that are bound together with duck, goose, or pork fat. It has a rich and flavoursome taste, thanks to garlic and herbs. Hardy and I lick our honey-and-duck-fat fingers, and take yet another sip of apple wine. Life is a chanson!

The Limousin is also famous for its nuts. Spiteful neighbours refer to us as the *mâcheurs de châtaignes* – the chestnut chewers. Chestnuts are a French obsession, and are served in a thousand different ways. Everything that has feathers is stuffed with them. Syrups, creams, sauces and even a wholly uncivilised liqueur are made with this fruit. Yes, it's actually a fruit, and not a nut! In French cuisine there is a distinct separation between fruit and nut mixes.

The three most popular incarnations in which the simple chestnut makes its appearance on the French table are as whole roasted chestnuts in a glass jar, as candied fruit or *marrons glacés*, and as the much-loved chestnut cream that has been sold in tins since the year dot. You spread the cream like butter on a brioche or a piece of toasted baguette. Or you mix a few spoons into your yoghurt. Or you do what I do: go and sit under the tree with the tin and eat it with a spoon.

I ate my first chestnut under the Eiffel Tower as a stubble-faced student. The wonderful aroma lured me to a man who was roasting them over his drum fire. He was wearing a beret and a woollen scarf, which looked as if his beloved had knitted it for him. I bought a newspaper cone full of steaming chestnuts. Shelling them with your bare hands is not easy, but I will never forget that first morsel on my tongue: something between butter, potato, walnut and angel's breath took over my mouth. I decided, right there, that I was going to spend part of my life there. C'est tout (and that's that).

On another occasion, we take a long detour to Provence to walk, among other things, in Vincent van Gogh's footsteps in Saint-Rémy-de-Provence. By 'we', I mean Ton and Anet, who join us with enthusiasm – Anet ever at the ready with her camera to document the odyssey for the offspring.

Saint-Rémy is a beautiful village in the heart of the Alpilles mountains. It is built upon one of Europe's oldest archaeological sites. The Romans named it Glanum; it's a site of Greek and Roman ruins. There are huge pine forests on the slopes of the Alpilles; until late in the afternoons, the cicadas play their concert in the trees. Nostradamus, the 16th-century astronomer, doctor and seer, was born in Saint-Rémy, and refers to its powerful magical forces.

For just over a year, Vincent van Gogh convalesced in a hospital outside Saint-Rémy under the watchful eye of Dr Théophile Peyron. He created 150 drawings and 143 paintings here, among the most compelling in his oeuvre. Initially, he only worked in and around the hospital's gardens and patios, but as he recovered he ventured further, through the olive and cypress stands, the wheatfields, the irises, the wildflowers.

Legend has it that, at a certain spot on one of his painting excursions, Vincent fell into a state of confusion, hearing voices speaking in Greek. He told his doctor about it in detail; the doctor had to give him an injection to calm him down.

When our spirited group is there, archaeologists have just excavated an agora, or marketplace. Among other things, it contains a library with books and parchment rolls – mostly in Greek. Was it the voices of long-departed Greeks that Vincent heard as he wandered through the cypresses?

Viewing paintings and locations open-mouthed is not all we do on this trip. We also laugh until the cicadas go quiet.

On our first night, we stay in a fancy hotel with a restaurant and a pale young chef who enchants people from near and far with her Mediterranean dishes. I'm running a bit late for dinner. Hardy, Anet and Ton are already having sundowners on the terrace, but I still need to shower.

I hang my new designer silk shirt over an unusual light in the passage: a wooden arm holding a flaming torch. The 'flame' is made of glass and covers the light bulb. I linger in the shower for a good while, until I smell something burning. When the smoke starts billowing in under the bathroom door, I rush out.

My shirt is in flames! It astounds me to this day that that glass torch could have given off enough heat to set my shirt on fire. Seconds later, a hell of a commotion erupts when the sprinkler system in the roof comes on. I enjoy a second shower – ice cold, this time, and apparently Windolene-flavoured.

Things happen very quickly after that. Staff members scramble in and around my room. I open the door that leads onto the garden, still in my birthday suit. Sometime later, a real beefcake brings me a damp towel to cover my shame.

I'm so thankful for the towel that, in front of a growing crowd of nosy parkers, I say to him, with inordinate gratitude, 'Je suis très content, je te baiser!'

What I mean to say, jokingly, is that I'm so grateful I could kiss him. 'Baiser' (the noun) means 'a kiss', but if you use it as a verb it means something like to 'roll in the hay' with someone. Quelle horreur!

Beefcake gives me just one look and says, 'Vous êtes bourré, monsieur!' (You are plastered, sir!) Talk about ingratitude. All I wanted was to show that I was thankful. 'Plastered' – without having had a single drink.

Later that night, a good many Boeings have flown over, their white contrails still burnt into the night sky. All I can do is wonder why so many of my well-intentioned attempts at being French devolve into such carnage.

# 18

# Louis spills the beans
# (well, just a few)

This chapter, with its steaming paragraphs about our château guests' amorous antics, spends a bit of time on our lawyer's desk before I hit send. To make doubly sure, my advocate friend also gives the silly stories a read-through, just to be sure that I'm not inadvertently stepping on anyone's toes. Or red-soled Louboutin heels.

Our guests come from all over the world – from South Africa too, of course. We could tell you stories that would make your hair stand on end. But most of them ended up in the lawyer's waste-paper basket.

Something else that ended up in the wastepaper basket was a few intimate, battery-operated toys that the pin-up with the red soles left in the bedside table. Weeks after they departed, her Scandinavian companion with the high voice asked in an email whether they'd perhaps left any of their 'sports equipment' behind in their room. We informed them that the chambermaid had thrown the whole caboodle, including the empty shopping bag, in the bin. We never heard from them again.

There are, however, one or two stories that the lawyer said I could share.

One night, we have to leave our guests on their own for a few hours after dinner to attend a function at the mairie. We put enough champagne and other drinks out for them to entertain themselves.

Walking up the stairs upon our return, we can already hear the commotion in the music room. It sounds like a stag party, despite the fact that the only people staying here at the moment are a few ladies from the Boland. Just as we slip past them to the calm of our apartment in the roof, it suddenly goes quiet.

Hardy looks at me. I look back at him, wide-eyed. Carefully, he turns the gold door handles to open the doors.

What we see looks just like a scene from the Lido de Paris. A showgirl lies on top of the piano, clad in nothing but a silver fox fur, her lovely legs in the air. Her ankles are elegantly crossed; there's a pair of patent leather heels on her petite little feet, like Marilyn Monroe's. The other guests are partying away, unconcerned about their companion's disinhibition.

A man dances alone in one corner of the salon, an imaginary partner in his outstretched arms. Wearing only a jacket and pants. Heaven only knows what happened to his shirt. An impeccably dressed couple *langarms* down the passage, while a clearly inebriated young man tries to push an upside-down CD into the CD player that's already playing.

Completely unfazed, Hardy opens another bottle of champagne. Without lifting an eyebrow, the lovely showgirl works her coat around her nakedness and takes a glass of the golden bubbles from Hardy. Pourquoi pas?

The themed tours that we offer at La Creuzette are in high demand. One of our beloved guests has been to La Creuzette five times, on a different tour each time. On one of our popular garden tours early in the year, we meet an exceptional woman of a certain age – a compelling woman, who has us spellbound at the dinner table every night with her colourful stories. She is a landscaper of renown and travels a lot. Her husband is a retired accountant who makes ceramic pots to order on a plot in the Klein Karoo.

On day three, our group visits the gardens of Notre-Dame d'Orsan, not far from Boussac. While Hardy is parking the van, the lady's phone rings. 'Ag, it's nothing urgent. It can wait.' She declines the call, and is just about to put it back into her bag when it rings again. This happens a good few times before she eventually takes the call. 'Yes,' she says sternly. 'I'm at home. I'm working in the garden.' She sits bolt upright, her eyes now as big as oranges. 'Okay, okay, I'll call back later. Bye . . .'

What happened is this: the lady did not feel like bringing her husband on the garden tour, so she came up with an inventive plan. On behalf of a made-up client, she ordered six massive ceramic pots from her husband (and paid for them). It would take him about the same time to make them as our garden tour. Give or take a day or two.

Hubby hits the high road to the Klein Karoo with a smile, happy that he's doing so well with his pots. He is apparently busy with his second pot when his electric potter's wheel gives up the ghost. It appears that it tripped the power in their farmhouse too. He loads the broken equipment into his car and starts the long trip back to the Cape to have it fixed. Before he drops it off at the factory, he decides to jump into the shower quickly at home.

'Where is Mevrou?' he asks the gardener, who paces around a little and clasps his hands.

'She is gone.'

'What do you mean, gone?'

'Gone, overseas.'

It takes a lot of sweet talking to calm him down. Both Hardy and I have to have a go. In the end, he admits that it's a funny story. His last words to me are, 'She could have just told me.'

At the table that night, I have to take over the storytelling for a while. But by the time the dessert and muscadel arrive, our landscaper is back on form. We decide to call her husband, with her iPhone on speakerphone. We all have a good laugh together, on two continents.

If my studio could talk, it would have a few interesting stories to tell. A few peculiar things have happened there; people get carried away, I suspect, by all the creative energy.

On one of our themed tours, the group is busy painting a boisterous bunch of bearded irises. Everyone is doing their preparatory sketches. I notice that one woman has her back turned to the still life, and that she is already painting. Everyone has been given an apron to wear, but she doesn't want to take off her lovely white jacket.

'This is how I always paint, neatly dressed and ready to go out,' she says.

The easels are on wheels, so that you can turn your work in any direction. I walk over to her and turn her easel, helpfully, to face

*Above and opposite, above:* My attic studio at La Creuzette and some of the guests who attended my art classes.

*Opposite, below:* Writer Riana Scheepers
(fourth from right) gave writing classes at La Creuzette and
was joined by radio presenter Amore Bekker (back row,
third from left), journalist Elmari Rautenbach (third from
right), writer Keina Swart (far right) and other guests.

Guests can also
take cooking
lessons at
La Creuzette.
Here, a group of
them are cooking
and concentrating
very hard in
our summer
kitchen.

the right way. 'Move your chair over this way, then you can carry on painting with an eye on the still life,' I say.

She looks at me as if I've made some kind of indecent proposal. Her glasses are speckled with grey paint. 'This is not how I work at home.'

I don't say anything about the grey and black strokes on her canvas. The irises are purple and blue, but I'm not going to interfere too much at this early stage; we could have a budding Picasso on our hands.

On a long table at one end of the studio, I've packed all the equipment and paint that the students might need. It's not long before the woman goes to investigate. She squeezes about half a cup of white paint out of the large tube, and is just about to do the same with the black tube.

'Good heavens,' I say. 'You could repaint the entire studio twice with that much. There's enough paint on your palette for four paintings. Please finish that first.'

She looks at me through glasses that, by now, are practically covered in grey fingerprints. She turns her easel away from the still life again. In the process, her neighbour's palette falls off the table. Without a word, she sits down with her back to the still life once again and starts to paint.

At teatime, everyone rolls their easels into a circle with their paintings facing inwards. We talk about their progress, and discuss any problems they may have encountered as they worked. Everyone's easel, except hers, is facing the right way.

'Please turn your easel this way?' I ask.

She knocks over her chair; her glasses fall off. She stands up, her white-jacketed back against the wet painting. When she steps away from her work, one of the students gives a loud snort behind me.

What she's painted is definitely not irises, nor flowers of any kind, but a grotesque figure of a man – in extravagant anatomical detail. In black and white. And grey. And no, she is *not* a budding Picasso.

'That is what I see,' she says, without batting an eyelid.

'Let me clean those glasses of yours with some turpentine,' I say softly.

'Thanks,' she says, and turns towards the window, her painting reproduced like a tattoo on the back of her jacket.


On one of the first food tours with our chef friend from Green Point, a very special group of women from the Boland comes to La Creuzette. There are ten or so of them, each one as lovely as the next. Almost all of them are farmers' wives; they know their Chenins from their Chardonnays, their Mourvèdres from their Petit Verdots.

'The handbrake's off,' says one of the women on the day they arrive. 'Our husbands are not around, and we feel like a bit of sport.'

I look to Hardy for support, but he's already pouring the first glass of champagne. 'Hoppa!' the woman in the sunglasses pipes up. 'Hoppa,' I say carefully, and take a long sip from my glass.

To make a very long story short, we split our sides laughing for most of that tour. The jokes and stories flowed like wine.

On an unexpectedly grey and rainy Sunday morning, the ladies have to get up at the crack of dawn for a visit to a large brocante in a neighbouring district. I decide to have bit of a lie-in. Later, I set the table in the summer kitchen with a tongue-in-cheek theme: I unpack all the brocante finds I'm not using onto a brightly coloured damask tablecloth.

There's a surprise among all the bric-a-brac: a little stuffed fox that one of our guests bought at a brocante and left behind – along with a wild boar's head – in our storeroom. At the Air France counter, when the time came to check the moth-eaten creatures in with her Louis Vuitton luggage, her courage beat a hasty retreat.

The sun puts in another appearance later that afternoon. It is wonderfully warm and cosy in the room that opens onto the stoep next to the summer kitchen. I'm expecting the guests in the next hour or so; Hardy always gives me a missed call so I can make sure I look presentable. I stretch out on the chaise longue and shut my eyes, just for a few moments. I yawn like I've never yawned before and drift, utterly content, on the warm wash of sunlight, all the way to dreamland.

I wake with a start to the fearsome sounds of a jackal's yelp and the long cry of wolves. For a moment, I think the fox on the table has come back to life. Then I see them, standing around the coffee table. Ten women in hairy coats. There's karakul, jackal, mink, hare, angora, alpaca, raccoon, chinchilla, beaver and something that looks like stray cat. There's been a sale at a well-known dealer who trades in second-hand furs. Our shivering guests, Hardy tells me, did not need a second invitation to procure a pelt.

What a festive table it was that night. There was much pelt-swapping and laughing – until one of the women started scratching her neck until red welts rose. We investigate; it is only when I put my glasses on that I see the tiny insects.

Chaos erupts at the table. It's truly the quickest striptease I have ever seen. Pelts fly through the air. The Malbec flows. As one, we shout, 'Hoppa!'

The pelts join the wild boar, and the poor little fox, on the top shelves of La Creuzette's storeroom. Hardy burns most of the pelts on a bonfire. I suspect that, before long, the remaining animals will follow.

# 19

## The fifth season

Autumn. Between September's giving way and December's solstice, a giver of golden life. Harvest time, pruning time. Time for the hunt.

Summer is over. The scent of autumn is sweet and smoky; in every garden, leaves and cuttings are burnt. On weekends, hunters in full regalia make their moves. On and off, the crack of a rifle.

October. Still the best month of all – here, and surely in the south, where it's spring. Boerneef articulates the season with so much feeling: 'Die najaar is nou op sy herfsste' (The autumn is now at its autumnest).

Standing under the massive plane trees with open arms, the leaves gently falling, is unreal. Nonpareil. It's like standing inside a snowglobe: enchanting, cut off from all the world. You're caught in a ochre moment whose colours burn.

While hatted hunters chase down buck and boar with Armagnac breaths, others slip through the forest with baskets, in search of juicy mushrooms. With a twinkle in the eye, the old people like to say that there are two ways to get rid of a spouse: a shooting accident, for the men, and mushroom poisoning, for the women. For every mouthwatering mushroom, there's a deadly doppelgänger.

When two cyclists and an old lady on her stoep are killed in separate hunting accidents, the French president issues a concerned – and urgent – request: during hunting season, don't loaf around on your stoep; and cycling is a dangerous sport that needs to be banned immediately.

Recently, a woman was gathering mushrooms when a shot rang out. The hunter who was responsible for the poor woman's demise was a former policeman whose hunting licence had expired.

In autumn, France becomes the crossroads for hundreds of types of migratory birds. The heavens teem with thousands of them. Imagine, in late October, 3 000 swallows settling in the trees overnight. The sound is indescribably magical. The chirping is one thing – but the sound of the multitude of wings! It's something between the wind sighing through the trees and a sharper sound, like paper being crumpled.

I run outside the minute I hear the unmistakable call of the cranes. Every time I see their splendour, it's as if my heart overflows. In that moment, I identify completely with nature and the animal kingdom. I understand why people become animal rights activists.

The common crane was once a threatened species, because so much of their habitat during the breeding and overwintering seasons is disturbed through construction projects and other abominations – not to mention the deaths from deadly poisons. Nonetheless, during their autumn migration these graceful migrants rest in France's Camargue, in the Rhône delta, before journeying on to Spain and North Africa. Their scientific name, *Grus grus*, sounds a great deal like their incessant calls when they are on the wing. The French call them *gris gris* (grey grey), a name that captures their call even better. They are demonstrably loud and social during the flight, which covers thousands of miles. They fly in a V formation that is something to behold. The leader is replaced every so often by another, eyes fixed on the wide horizon – there where, far ahead, the summer sun shines.

When winter comes to the north and summer puts in an appearance in the south, we do just what the cranes do: follow the sun. Call it instinct, call it indulgence: Hardy wants to put a snoek on the fire, and I want to see how my spekbooms are doing, next to the dune at our house on the West Coast.

Hardy and I are obsessed with this bleached, secluded coast. We've been renting holiday homes there for years, but always seem to return to a specific house – in a private nature reserve on a peninsula just past Britannia Bay. As the coastline goes, Paternoster is about 20 km further along.

The erstwhile owners of the reserve kept a few plots aside for family who still wanted to build there. The loveliest plot belongs to the son-in-law, whose house we rent so often. It's almost on the head of the peninsula, and has a panoramic view that takes your breath away. You see three strips of sea: St Helena Bay, Kaloenie se Baai right in front of the house, and Britannia Bay. The sun rises and sets over the same horizon. Go and look it up – it's true! It is a paradise, this place. When the plot went up for sale, we bought it instantly, even though we didn't really want to own property in South Africa again. Less is more, as my mother used to say.

It takes us a year to decide on the design for the house. When, eventually, it is built, we decide to incorporate something from France – so that we don't miss it too much while we're there. A huge chandelier hangs over the dining room table, and on the wall is a tapestry that was woven in the same decade as Jan van Riebeeck came ashore.

It's also a house filled with light, but it's the antithesis of La Creuzette. The beach house is modern and open. I paint the interior spaces the same smoky quartz colour as those of La Creuzette. The name of the colour – karma – satisfies my sense of the poetic.

It feels like our lives are in perfect balance. When we're in South Africa, we're there with heart and soul. When we're in France, we're there with heart and soul, too. I found it difficult to leave France when we came to South Africa on our most recent visit. I am busy with this book, and with a series of forest scenes in my studio at the same time. The departure date catches up with me all too soon. I become that grumpy traveller who keeps looking back; my beloved French home becomes ever smaller on the horizon.

It's late afternoon when we arrive at the West Coast. My heart is still heavy; I'm finding fault with everything around me. Hardy rolls up the blinds and pushes the concertina doors open all the way. Kaloenie se Baai. On its aquamarine horizon, the breath of a large pod of whales is made visible. My heart softens. I am home.

Our feet are firmly anchored on two continents, Africa and Europe. Two loves. Two homes.


A few years ago, we decided to apply for French citizenship. There are many reasons for this. One is that it will simplify the red tape and complexity surrounding income tax and other taxes in France.

The French bureaucracy's great love of paperwork is universally known. Their system has to be the most complicated in the world.

I have an instant aversion to the piles of forms in nine-point Helvetica that are slid in front of us. French forms. Luckily, Hardy has a cool head. He sighs deeply, then tackles the impossible task line by line. As for me, I look out the window, watching the autumn leaves fall.

*Les fonctionnaires* (civil servants), the pillars of the state bureaucracy, are a breed of their own. They worship every letter of the law. And each one in the office wants things done a different way. If you can accept and handle that, you've won the battle. You're almost French. Like us.

When we've tracked down the scores of documents we need for our citizenship application, and had them all issued, I'm ready to throw in the towel. Tracking down my parents' birth certificates – originals, mind you – was a real challenge. A short story of its own hides herein.

In addition, all the papers need to be translated by an official translator. The whole business takes 18 months. Seconds before the clock strikes midnight and my whole life turns into a pumpkin, our dossier is approved. The last step is an interview with the senior state official in the region.

I have my hair cut and shine my shoes until I can see the Eiffel Tower reflecting in them. At first light we make for Guéret, the seat of the prefect in charge of the Creuse. The trip reminds me of my childhood, and our annual exodus to Durban for the July holidays, my fringe neatly Brylcreemed out of my eyes. All that's missing is Ma's basket of *padkos*.

215

We're an hour or so early, of course. We sit on a damp bench in the park and watch the squirrels – and fonctionnaires – scamper across the paved pathways. At the appointed time we find ourselves in a dull official waiting room. I know that state department waiting rooms aren't particularly attractive anywhere in the world, but *vaderland*, are we not in the land of Dior and Art Deco?

A bland secretary records our attendance in a massive red file. With a fountain pen, no less; she screws the lid shut after having to write out my long, complicated surname twice. She wears her hair in an old-fashioned beehive and looks tired and livid.

We sit next to each other on a bench upholstered in yellow leatherette that creaks every time we move. I wipe the dust from the park off one shiny shoe and then another, while reminding Hardy that he promised to repeat all the difficult questions – the ones with figures and dates – out loud, in Afrikaans, as if he is reflecting on them aloud before he answers them.

People have warned us that they pepper you with questions about historical dates and difficult political concerns. Liberté, égalité, fraternité, all that stuff. The receptionist announces that it is time. Hardy and I shoot over to the dark door at the end of the awful room.

'Non, non!' the beehive screeches, her lips drawn paperclip-thin. 'Un à la fois, s'il vous plaît!' (One at a time, please!)

Crisis: I'm going to have to manage on my own. I push Hardy out of the way and rip the door open. It's now or never.

A madame sits behind an impressive desk. Two phones: one black, one red. I can't help thinking about James Bond in M's office. Behind the madame, two national flags, draped very dramatically, betraying a hint of national taste. I sit on the edge of the appointed seat. My throat is like the Kalahari desert.

Her designer French glasses make her taut face almost lovely. She struggles with my surname, swallows the makings of a laugh and smiles indulgently in my direction. 'Vous êtes un artiste?' (You are an artist?) she asks, back in control.

My grandfather used to say that one should always shoot first. Her words have not yet gone cold when I let loose with a nice little salvo about my favourite French painters and museums. When she tries to get a word in edgeways, I forge on, unrelenting, with my elaborate paean to Paris and our fertile Limousin region.

Madame tries once or twice more, but I keep on – about French singers and their beautiful songs. I pronounce their names expertly, and with nuance: Charles Aznavour, Mireille Mathieu, Hélène Ségara. When I start to go on about Brigitte Bardot, she holds up her hand. Her nails are as red as pomegranates.

'You seem to be a cultivated person,' she says, looking at her watch. I lean back in my seat, tasting victory in a mouth that's no longer quite so dry. All my chattering has made an oasis of the desert. I lean back even further, as if I'm at the bioscope.

Hardy looks at me questioningly as I walk past him. I smile happily. 'C'est du tout cuit' (That was a piece of cake), I whisper gallantly.

A very long while later, Hardy exits through the dark door, looking ragged. In his interview, the madame worked studiously through every question on her list. From Louis XIV to President Sarkozy. Dates, figures, everything. He keeps quiet almost all the way home.

'We're almost French,' he says, finally breaking the silence. When he high-fives me, he nearly drives the car off the road.

At a glamorous event in the mairie, a troop of big knobs hands your citizenship over to you. The mayor must also attend the ceremony, in all his regalia. What a spectacle.

And so it is that, suited and tied, our hair combed back neatly once again, we find ourselves on the winding stairs of the mairie with our French friend and mayor. In his Tricolore sash, he shakes his new fellow citizens' hands proudly while the band plays 'La Marseillaise'. There's a lump in my throat; my eyes are burning. That is how, in 2010, we become Frenchmen.

And yet, when the days turn pale around the gills and the mercury dips below freezing, we close the shutters tightly and lock the big iron gate for a while. As the first snowflakes fall, we do as the birds do: fly south. To the West Coast, where I breathe a little differently.

# 20

# 'J'ai deux amours, mon pays et Paris'

i

15 April 2019

It's twenty past six on a cobalt-blue spring morning in April and I'm standing on one of my favourite bridges in Paris – the Pont Neuf, the city's oldest bridge. In the old days, the pavements would have been packed with stalls and kiosks selling anything from brightly coloured ribbons to knives. Fortune tellers and tooth-pullers would have been on hand to redeem you of your pain or sadness, for a fee.

I'm very fond of bridges. It must be because my father used to carry me on his shoulders over the bridge at Victoria Falls. A bridge represents adventure. Do some reading up about the unbelievable living bridges of Cherrapunji in India, which are over 500 years old. It is pure joy to stand on the bridge that spans the Petite Creuse, just outside Boussac, and to soak your thoughts in water.

The 29 bridges that cross the Seine in Paris offer 29 moments of meditation. I look in the direction of the next bridge, the more modern Pont des Arts. To my left is the impressive Institut de France, with its exquisite dome and gilded decorations. To my right is the Louvre, with its astonishing collection of art treasures.

As your gaze follows the Seine, you take in the Eiffel Tower on the horizon, and the contrast between the modern architecture of La Défense and the Arc de Triomphe at the top of the Champs-Élysées. This place is very dear to me. As a student, I stood here and dreamt; as a struggling artist, I sought relief. And, these days, gazing out over Paris from this bridge is a kind of homecoming.

Contrails criss-cross the blue sky to remind me that Paris is a world city. When I turn around and cross over to the pavement on the opposite side, I see how the Seine splits to form the two islands, Île de la Cité and Île Saint-Louis.

The word 'beautiful' is almost inadequate for this tableau. The Conciergerie, with its grey turrets – where Marie Antoinette was held for a while during the revolution – is on the right, the spire of Notre Dame Cathedral clearly visible. The last mist of the day is almost gone.

A fire alarm goes off in the roof of the cathedral. The organ music is abandoned; overwhelmed tourists and tour guides are bundled outside. Someone goes to investigate, but finds nothing in the antique wooden eaves. Twenty-five minutes later, a second alarm goes off. The stately cathedral's heavy wooden doors have already been closed; the interior is empty, save for the scurrying officials.

The antique roof trusses are known as 'the forest'. They burn, now, just as a forest would burn. Wooden beams that date from the twelfth and thirteenth centuries char like paper in the flames.

People watch from the banks of the Seine, aghast. Cellphone cameras flicker and flash in the dusk. A vicious wind picks up. A young woman falls to her knees, hands clasped in prayer. Somewhere, someone is weeping. Firefighters pump arcs of water from the river. The iconic polychromatic wooden spire burns like a massive candle from the Middle Ages. There is something apocalyptic about the scene.

The 91-metre-high spire gives. It plummets through the smoke and soot, right through the ceiling, into the cathedral's glowing nave. Embers rain like confetti from the sky. A crooked line of firefighters, officials and other helpers forms, to ferry the most important treasures out of the church. The human chain passes holy reliquaries, hand to hand, to the waiting police vehicles whose blue lights make flashing halos. The holy crown of thorns is carried out on a stretcher, before the watchful eyes of the crowd. Thunderous applause breaks out – a biblical son et lumière show.

Notre Dame is a Gothic wonder that has watched over Paris and its people for almost 800 years. Its construction began in 1163, when Pope Alexander III laid the first cornerstone. It was consecrated in 1345, with great fanfare. It was not the monarchy's most favoured place of worship, however; this honour fell to Reims Cathedral and the Basilica of Saint-Denis. Instead, Notre Dame was the cathedral of the everyman.

Over the centuries, Notre Dame fell into disrepair, especially after large-scale plundering during the French Revolution. In 1831, Victor Hugo published his novel *Notre-Dame de Paris*, known in English as *The Hunchback of Notre Dame*. It captured the imagination of the public; its main characters, Quasimodo and Esmeralda, focused attention back onto the church. A comprehensive restoration project, under renowned architect Viollet-le-Duc, was launched. A few years ago, the musical *Notre-Dame de Paris*, based loosely on Hugo's novel, returned to the stage. It was a runaway success.

It's impossible to talk about Notre Dame and Quasimodo with-out at least mentioning the cathedral's legendary bells. There were originally ten bronze bells. Some were melted down to make can-nons during the revolution. Mercifully, the largest one – bourdon Emmanuel – escaped unharmed. It does weigh 13 tons, after all.

In 1856, four main bells entered service and have chimed every 15 minutes, without exception, ever since. They heralded the end of the First World War, and the liberation of Paris in 1944. They are part of the Parisian ambience, and have their own names: Angélique-Françoise, Antoinette-Charlotte, Hyacinthe-Jeanne and Denise-David.

In 1999, there was talk of replacing these beloved residents of the tower with new ones that would peal just like the original 17th-century bells. The announcement made waves in the city. Many Parisians felt that the 19th-century bells were as much a part of the city's literary history as Hugo's famous hunchbacked bell-ringer.

Now, the bells have fallen silent. No one knows how long the silence will endure, but there are scores of avant-garde designs for a new roof and tower on the drawing boards of the world's foremost architects. Donations for the restoration are streaming in from all over the world. The French president has vowed that the beloved Notre Dame will be returned to its people, albeit in a new incarnation, as soon as possible.

The magnificent rose window survived the flames, thankfully. What moved me deeply is that three of the historic beehives on the roof also survived. It made front-page news that the bees were still there, and still producing honey. Life goes on.

On a lighter note, but still on the theme of the cathedral's wonderful rose window, allow me to tell a story from long ago – 1980, to be exact. It's Christmas Eve in Paris. It had snowed earlier that morning; the city looks like a hand-painted Christmas card. I'm a little sad, as this time I'm alone in Paris. Not that you can't be alone in Paris, but it's Christmas and I'm far from home.

The women are in fox fur against the worst of the winter bite. I smell the sweet scent of cinnamon and the resin of felled pines. Children's hands in little woollen gloves grasp at everything that glitters in the beautifully lit shop windows. I cross the bridge to the Île Saint-Louis; I want to go and sit in the cathedral. There, in the dusky light, one can see reason: I have weighty decisions to make.

There's a hell of a crowd in the impressive square in front of the church. Georges-Eugène Haussmann, who rebuilt Paris under Napoleon III, designed the square specifically so that Parisians could gather in front of their beloved church. I climb the railing of the bridge and hang on to a lamppost. I look out over the people's heads and see a ray of light switch on inside the cathedral. It shines through the rose window, over the crowd, bathing them in a colourful aquarelle. Music starts to play; Joan Baez sings, 'How many roads must a man walk down ...'

## ii

'J'ai deux amours, mon pays et Paris' is a song about two loves: one for your country, and one for Paris. I have not deux amours, but trois: the West Coast, France and Paris!

It is practically impossible to write about Paris. Where do you start? And end? Since my dreams about Paris began on the Pont Neuf, I'll take a walk through the first arrondissement alone.

It's a short walk across the bridge and left along the Quai du Louvre to the Rue de l'Amiral de Coligny – the street that runs along the side of the Louvre. Roughly across from the Cour Carrée, at number six, is the well-known brasserie Le Fumoir – one of the trendiest hangouts for drinks and light meals by day. By night, it's more formal, and very popular for dinner – so book well in advance if you want a table.

Le Fumoir is a chic, relaxed, noisy place, where the people from the neighbourhood meet to socialise. Or to enjoy a quiet noisette on their own, with a viennoiserie, while paging through a large selection of international magazines and newspapers.

Let's take the Rue de Rivoli to the Palais-Royal, once a royal palace and hands down my favourite building and garden in Paris. The garden, with its avenues of neatly pruned plane trees and central fountain, is a real French oasis in this big city. A range of royals and dignitaries have lived here, from Cardinal Richelieu to King

Louis XIII and his widow, Anne of Austria. It has also been the palace of Louis Philippe II, the Duke of Orléans.

The Comédie Française, one of the first state theatres in France, is part of the architectural façade through which you enter the hyper-modern courtyard, the heart of the Palais-Royal.

Perhaps I should mention that my devotion to the shops and culinary magic at the Palais-Royal influences my impressions of it. A colonnade runs all the way around the courtyard, which contains the Orléans and Vallois galleries. Some of the boutiques here have existed for centuries; it's here that you'll spot some of the best-dressed women in Paris. Just take a seat on one of the dark-green park benches and wait. You'll see.

Ah, better still, go and enjoy a little something at one of the open-air cafés. My favourite is the Café Palais-Royal – restrained and extravagant in equal measure. They make a fish-and-chips dish with a playfully modern twist – the fish is fried inside a small loaf of bread with the potato chips inside, just like a chip roll! A glass of chilled Beaumes-de-Venise under the grey-and-white-striped umbrellas rounds it all off.

If you're feeling brave, book a table for two at the window at Le Grand Véfour. Superchef Guy Martin will take you on a culinary tour to places where your taste buds have never ventured. Your wallet is guaranteed to protest, but remember: it's only money.

The Palais-Royal embodies the city's storied past. In direct contrast are the Rue de Rivoli and the Rue du Faubourg Saint-Honoré, with all their glamorous shops. In the arcades of the Palais-Royal you'll find another string of shops, boutiques and galleries that will keep you busy for at least an hour or three. There's a tiny shop,

My shop, Le Store, on the town square of Boussac.

With a few models in front of the shop.

for example, filled with antique and modern music boxes – from the exotic, miniature Napoleon III pianos to modern matchbox players that cost only a few euros and play songs like 'La Vie en rose' and 'L'Heure bleue'.

A few shops further along is the famous La Petite Robe Noire, a popular shop that sells second-hand vintage designer dresses, all of them black: Dior, Balenciaga, Worth, Saint Laurent and Givenchy, from the 1950s, 1960s and 1970s. Vanessa Paradis and Sophie Marceau are often spotted there.

From Salons du Palais-Royal Shiseido, a shop or two further down, Catherine Deneuve collects a perfume – in a hand-cut crystal bottle – that's been mixed for her alone by master perfumier Serge Lutens. If it's good enough for Queen Noor of Jordan, it's probably good enough for you! It's cheaper than you think, and the shop is a real experience – especially the salesladies, who look as if they belong in a Claude Chabrol film.

See how the Palais-Royal has waylaid me? We haven't made it to a fraction of my favourite places in the first arrondissement.

All I can do is leave you with a list of my other favourites. For lunch or a light supper, Café Marly on the veranda of the Louvre. You might even run into Isabelle Huppert or Marion Cotillard.

At least once a month, I have to pop in at Astier de Villatte, the homeware shop. It's small and – as is typically French – modest, but have a good look at the shabby-looking crockery. You'll find handmade cups and jugs with crooked handles that have been finished on the inside with 22-carat gold or platinum!

La Bovida is in the Rue Montmartre, near the old Les Halles market. Like the nearby E. Dehillerin, it's a double-storey corner shop that sells everything you can imagine for the kitchen. These two shops are an absolute must for food fundis. It's here that you'll find your Laguiole knives, or that new stainless steel mandoline.

In the Rue Hérold, you'll find one of Paris's ground-breaking boutiques: Leclaireur. It has the latest decor on show long before it's copied by the style editors of the glossy magazines. It also sells clothes by young designers. It's the heartbeat of Paris's creative youth, and will introduce you to contemporary Dutch designers too.

Then there are the bookshops. Let me begin with the most basic – *les bouquinistes*, over 250 of them. These are booksellers who sell their wares on both sides of the Seine from riverside book kiosks: new and old books, rare first editions, comic books and black-and-white postcards of old castles and film stars.

There are about 169 bookshops in the fifth arrondissement alone. In 1981, regulations governing book sales, known as the 'loi Lang' (after Jack Lang, then minister of culture), were enacted. According to the regulations, the publisher sets the selling price of a book and all shops have to sell that book for the same amount. In special cases, a discount of five per cent is permitted. It's a law that keeps small family businesses in the black, and prevents the big groups from dominating the market. You'll almost never find a three-for-two offer in French bookshops.

Librairie Galignani is one of my favourite bookshops in Paris. The family has been making a living from books since 1520; Simone Galignani printed one of the first books, in Venice, on the newly designed printing press. At the end of the 17th century, Giovanni Antonio Galignani moved to Paris, where he opened a bookshop in the Rue Vivienne. He also set up a reading room where people could read English texts as well. And he published a newspaper in which work by Byron, Wordsworth and Thackeray appeared. In 1856, the bookshop moved to a new address, in the Rue de Rivoli – Giovanni's descendants still sell books there. I can spend hours in Galignani: the smell of the books, the creaking of the wooden floor, the privilege of just being able to browse there.

Another nice place to browse is Shakespeare and Company, on the Rue de la Bûcherie, just across the way from Notre Dame. It is named after the celebrated bookshop in the Rue de l'Odéon established by Sylvia Beach, an American expatriate. Beach published James Joyce's *Ulysses* and promoted the work of Ernest Hemingway, Ezra Pound and Gertrude Stein. Today's Shakespeare and Company is managed by Sylvia Whitman, whose father, George, established the shop in 1964; just the other day, our very own J.M. Coetzee gave a reading there.

But let me stop there. I'm not even a quarter of the way through my list, but that's Paris for you: every step, every turn of the head, is an experience. You haven't heard me getting romantic about how the colour of the river changes at sunset, or what the first notes of Saint-Saëns' organ concerto sound like in the nave of L'église Saint-Eustache.

I'm on the Pont des Arts now. The sun is setting quickly; the musicians, artists and students are already starting their festivities on the bridge. Here, a fife and a violin; there, a guitar and a mouth organ. Everywhere, bottles of red wine, open. And champagne, of course.

Paris. Avenues of plane trees; fountains, hidden gardens, parks full of coolness and secret encounters. Churches and cathedrals and squares with gilded phantoms. Heroes, rulers and angels of tarnished bronze. Domes and attics full of people, cafés and bars and windows full of reflections. Hooters and sirens and the click-clack of heels. Love, and also suffering.

Paris is all this, and more. A young opera student stands on a corner and sings an aria from Gounod's *Roméo et Juliette*. 'Je veux vivre dans le rêve': I want to live in this dream.

# 21

## Where the plum tree blooms

'We'd like to ask you something, but it's okay if you don't want to.'

The woman, one of our guests, spreads fig jam on her croissant and takes a bite. There are crumbs everywhere. There's an art to eating a croissant. For starters, you don't cut the thing open like a laboratory frog. Whatever you want to put on the unsuspecting little bread, you plaster on top of it. You spread your jam on its brown-baked back and to hell with that sandwiching business.

She takes a sip of coffee from an oversized porcelain cup and looks at her husband, who rests his hand on her knee. 'Bennie and I could not get a moment's rest last night.'

*Is there something wrong with the room?* I wonder, anxious. Or is the lady allergic to the goose down in the pillows? Would she prefer a pillow made of organic Crimplene? We have some in our allergy cupboard. We have a few strange things in that cupboard, in fact – but that's a story for another day.

She dusts a few crumbs off her serviette. 'If you and Hardy don't mind, we'd also really like a house in Boussac.'

She looks down at her hands in her lap as if she's just revealed the most intimate thing. Maybe she has!

We know this croissant dance by heart. Hardy usually pulls his chair a little closer and starts explaining exactly what buying a house in France involves. After the first few minutes, I get bored and head for my studio to get a few brushstrokes in before teatime.

To date, 25 South African couples have made our lovely village their home. Some came and went, but most have become Boussacains. In season, you hear as much Afrikaans on the bistro stoeps as French. It gets festive, then. Look, we know how to *kuier*, as evidenced by that one Bastille Day when we had as many South African guests as French ones in the garden. When the French jazz band started packing up at one in the morning, I put an Amanda Strydom CD on; we danced till dawn on the wooden dance floor in front of what was once the stables.

The homes they buy are so vastly different that they deserve their own TV show. There are, literally and figuratively, houses, palaces and a pigsty or two – transformed into a Beatrix Potter fantasy through talent and plain hard work. There are watermills, a 17th-century townhouse, a gorgeous manor house with stained-glass windows that take your breath away, and a Renaissance castle with a drawbridge. I kid you not!

Of course, the South Africans' restoration work has spawned a sackful of stories. Ankles have been sprained; a finger has even been broken. But the language struggles still yield the funniest stories.

And don't think for a minute that two visits to the French equivalent of Builders Warehouse are going to do the trick. No, my friend. You are in for the long haul with the plumber and the electrician. As in South Africa, they are wide-eyed and full of promises in the beginning. When you've paid the deposit, they usually disappear for a few weeks. Just before you show up at your unsuspecting plumber's house with your loaded .303, he appears – with your basin, taps and toilet seat.

In a small village like Boussac, the plumber and electrician are on equal footing with the notary and the doctor. Just before Christmas, you give them a jug of tinned confit de canard or the best cognac you can afford. This substantially increases your chances of their replying to your urgent SMSes.

When the time comes to furnish their homes, most new residents use the Sunday brocante as a hunting ground for bargains. Some furnish their homes entirely with the purchases they make at the brocantes. The loveliest oak armoires replace ugly white built-in cupboards. Take it from me: it's a labour of love to oil your new oak wardrobe yourself, as you would the body of a beloved.

A friend of ours opened an art gallery. In the season, she offers one or two carefully curated exhibitions. It's become such an institution that the mayor opens her summer exhibition.

The village organises annual music concerts in the church, under the auspices of the mayoral couple. We decide to make a musical contribution to our community too. We usually start with a small, intimate recital in the music room at La Creuzette for our own guests and a selection of people from the village.

We then present a performance by South African artists in the church, which is open to the public. The Catholic church, with its beautiful stained-glass windows, is usually chock-full. Stars such as the mezzo-soprano Minette du Toit-Pearce, chanteur Niël Rademan and the legendary pianist Ilse Schumann have all brought the audience to their feet.

I will never forget Minette's well-rounded voice when she sang the aria from Saint-Saëns' *Samson et Dalila*: 'Mon cœur s'ouvre à ta voix' (My heart opens to your voice). I wiped my tears and sprang to my feet as she sang the final notes.

Because Frédéric Chopin lived near Boussac, the annual international Chopin festival is held in Nohant. Everyone in the area is a Chopin expert; don't even think about messing with their hero. One year, Ilse Schumann rehearsed Chopin's near-unplayable Piano Sonata No 3 for a full week. The magic began the moment she slipped in behind the piano in her midnight-blue gown and played the first notes, confidently and with heavenly compassion. She concluded the sonata with a jubilant finale. When she'd finished, her masterful phrasing lingered in the air for a moment before being engulfed by a thunderous ovation.

One summer, Amanda Strydom, a friend from years back, and her accompanist, Coenraad, perform a few concerts at La Creuzette. What fun it is. We empty the grand salon, and open the interleading doors to the dining room. The grand piano is moved in front of the music room's double doors, next to the grand salon. The music room and dining room are filled with chairs. Amanda sings everything from Piaf to Brel, Aucamp to Kerkorrel. She sings vintage Strydom, and brand-new Strydom. Seeing our French friends rocking with us in our language makes me glow.

In 2014, the authoritative *Figaro Magazine* names La Creuzette as one of the best guesthouses in the French countryside. I'll go so far as saying that Boussac experiences a second golden age at this time, a mini-Renaissance.

Hardy and my French adventure began 21 years ago. In the intervening years, we've often reflected, a bubbling glass of champagne in our calloused hands, on those kaleidoscopic early years in France. Years full of chance and excitement.

In the midst of it all, the mood takes me to write a book about our comings and goings in France – specifically at La Creuzette. Something between *What the Butler Saw* and 'Louis Spills the Beans'. This book is our dream made manifest.

La Creuzette will always be my first love. Living anywhere else had long been unthinkable. Yet, as the years passed, living in our 'office' became increasingly uncomfortable; four years ago, we decided to sell Château de la Creuzette – though with the undertaking to remain the custodians of this extraordinary home for a time.

La Creuzette continues to excel; the squadron of creative people at its helm is taking it to new heights. DeVerra and her Antonin now live at La Creuzette in a newly created *petite demeure* (small residence). She is still an irreplaceable right hand.

All of which meant – you guessed it – looking for a new place to live. Moving away was never a consideration – the area and its people are in our blood. 'Deep France' is the only place on earth where we want to hang up our aprons, brushes and hats for good.

The wheel of life turns in all manner of magical ways. And so it is that we draw to a halt at an address we'd lingered at, years ago, for the briefest moment. Our destination has no number, just a name: Le Rembucher.

I've learnt that, in my life, destiny and I run flat into each other at every turn. I used to fight it, but now I know that it's better to play along and watch your life unfold like a treasure hunt. Go with the flow.

The day I first see Le Rembucher is 'deur die blare', as we say in Afrikaans – literally, 'through the leaves', as was my first glimpse of the place, and figuratively, having a mind that's not clear. It is on that spring day when I've taken Hardy to show him where the Gypsies have discarded our concrete statues in the forest at Lépaud.

Popular singer Amanda Strydom
delivers a tour de force with her
accompanist, Coenraad Rall.

*Opposite:* Minette du Toit-Pearce and Niël Rademan
perform in Boussac's church.

I want to go for a walk in the forest, but Hardy is full of adventure. He takes me on an unplanned reconnaissance mission to the ruins of a nearby castle. It's not long before we're jumping like klipspringers among the sandstone blocks of Château de Lépaud.

Château de Lépaud is a flamboyant Renaissance castle that was built centuries ago for the princes of Chambon and Combraille, and the dukes of Orléans. In due course it fell into ruin, but was restored in the 17th century for Princess Anne Marie Louise d'Orléans, also known as La Grande Mademoiselle de France.

The princess's mother lived for only five days after her daughter's birth in 1627. Her father, Gaston, was the Duke of Orléans, and Louis XIII's oldest surviving brother. The week-old baby girl became the new Duchess of Montpensier, inheriting the most fabled fortune in Europe – including the duchy of Auvergne, along with the Château de Lépaud.

The impressive estate with its castle and outbuildings was referred to as the Château Royale. During the French Revolution, the complex was badly damaged. In time, it fell into ruin once more.

Every year, scores of important buildings in France turn to dust, purely because it is impossible for the French government to maintain them all. As I mentioned earlier, there are over a thousand châteaux in our region alone. Were it not for private initiatives that have resurrected a few of the structures, little more than a heap of stones would remain of them.

Part of the property was later subdivided and sold. During the 18th and 19th centuries, various restoration projects were launched, but it was only in the early 20th century that the heiress made large-scale changes to the buildings and modernised them. Mercifully, the 75-hectare forest came off more or less unscathed.

The forest is something of a legend; since the time of the princes of Orléans, it's been known as a hunter's paradise. It contains many types of deer, but is best known for its fabled wild boar – among the largest and most dangerous in France. One branch of the Orléans family uses the wild boar as an emblem in its heraldry.

When Hardy stops at the ruin of Château de Lépaud, we have a quick look at where the Gypsies made camp with our statues. Empty wine bottles and other rubbish are strewn around. He's in an incredible rush, as if something is urging him on to the castle. One imposing tower and part of the façade is still intact. It looks as if someone is making repairs: there are neat rows of bricks, and fragments of elaborate stonework.

We walk up to a beautifully decorated stone window frame. This, we learn later, is the building's only surviving Renaissance detail.

'Just look how seductively that plum tree is blooming,' Hardy says, walking up to the centuries-old tree. I join him, break off a little branch of blossoms and put it into the breast pocket of my jacket. I feel like a bridegroom.

It smells of spring and rain. The tree's wide branches are a white umbrella, gathering us in. A bright bird flutters from under the branches. 'Quel oiseau magnifique!' (What a magnificent bird!) Hardy says.

Before I can respond, he nudges me. 'Look!'

I turn around and look where Hardy is pointing. His index finger is aimed at the forest behind the château. At first, I don't see anything. It's a massive forest, the trees full of extravagant yellow-green spring leaves.

Then I see it: through the leaves, the pediment of a building. The new leaves rustle in the rising wind.

We don't go any closer to investigate, that day. But we're curious; we decide to make enquiries in Boussac.

'That is the hunting pavilion of the Château de Lépaud,' the auntie in the village café tells us. I've come in search of warmth, Hardy in search of coffee. Her hair is bundled up on her head, the bun held in place with a broken purple knitting needle. She smells of sugar and cinnamon.

'The owners of the castle sold that part of the estate years ago,' she says, putting the cup of coffee down in front of Hardy. 'It's called Le Rembucher.' She wipes her hands on her floury apron and stands with her hands on her hips, looking at us as if she expects us to come out with something magical.

It's raining outside. The landscape becomes a hazy watercolour through the café windows. In the distance, a glimpse of dark forest, etched against the sky.

The hipster estate agent cannot believe his ears when Hardy leaves a message for him to call us urgently.

''Allo meester 'Ardy, you looking for me?'

'Yes, sir, we are indeed.'

The game starts. Hardy makes a cheeky offer on Le Rembucher, which the agent conveys to the seller. I chew my nails almost to their moons.

Two days later, he calls back. 'If you meets us halfway weez zee price, you have youzelf a deal.'

The next day, we're sitting in his office signing the *compromis de vente* (offer to purchase). We meet again a few days later, in the agent's office. I see he's wearing a new, more expensive watch.

We sign the contract of sale and shake hands – with the agent, his handy secretary in her patent leather high-heeled sandals, the owner with the good-natured face. The back-slapping and air-kissing done, we drive our ample impatience and giant bunch of keys to our new house.

Hardy stops at a liquor store for a bottle of champagne and two glasses. And there, on the stoep of the hunter's pavilion outside Lépaud, the champagne cork arcs through the air and lands with a clang against the formidable iron gates that lead into the forest.

In 2001, we took on the massive restoration project that was La Creuzette with daring, and with stars in our eyes. By the time we start on Le Rembucher, the stars and the daring are still there. But we're older – and, mercifully, a little wiser.

The magical forest at the Le Rembucher estate.

The hunting pavilion of Le Rembucher,
which we call home these days.

*Opposite:* The majestic fireplace in our sitting room.
The doors open to the outside.

# Épilogue

For me, all roads led – eventually – to France, after all. The sound-track to the French scene that is still playing out in my life is Édith Piaf's: 'Non, je ne regrette rien.'

It's 21 years since we bought the little house in the crooked Lapeyrouse street. We celebrate the coming of age of our life in France, as we did at the start, with a salute from an ice-cold bottle of Bollinger Champagne Millésime. Its vintage? 1999, the same year in which we first set foot in la France profonde.

After two decades, we know how to propose a toast without hesitation – and how to respond to one appropriately. 'À votre santé!' we proclaim.

The two decades we've spent in France feel like the mere blink of an eye. But after so long, one can't help asking the inevitable question: how are we different now? Have things changed – and, if so, for better or for worse?

There have been four presidents in France in the past two decades: Jacques Chirac, Nicolas Sarkozy, François Hollande and currently Emmanuel Macron. We have something of a claim to fame in the presidential arena, albeit a bit tenuous. One of our friends, who also lives in the Lépaud district (in a beautiful château), is Bernadette Chirac's sister-in-law. She is elegant, the embodiment, to me, of a sophisticated French woman. Chic and understated.

One day, a few years ago, we are in a state: a letter from the Élysée Palace in Paris has come – on the official letterhead and everything. I hold my breath and open the letter very carefully. It's addressed to me and Hardy, and signed at the bottom in ink: With best wishes, Carla Bruni Sarkozy.

In 2010, we published the book *Festive France: Lifestyle and Cuisine from the French Countryside* with Anet. She gave a sample of the book to a South African youngster who knew Madame Sarkozy personally, and threatened him with death if he did not hand it to her himself. Ta-da! A letter of thanks from the elegant singer and first lady.

The letter graces our fridge for a good while, held in place by a Mandela fridge magnet. *Bah, dis donc!* (Well, you don't say!) If I don't rein myself in, I'll ben-dis-donc indefinitely. We don't have a story to tell about Hollande, our Hollandse origins aside. We're still working hard on a Macron story.

I'm still amazed by the rich French vocabulary. There's a word or three for every object, feeling and natural phenomenon. One of my favourites, which rolls so beautifully off the tongue, is *le va-et-vient*, the coming and going of things.

So what else has changed in the past two decades? The price of a cup of coffee, for one thing. This makes the French antsy: coffee is a national institution that is best left unmolested. It is rumoured that you'll pay anything from four to seven euros for a small cup of black coffee in Paris. Which is true, depending on where in Paris you go to seek your solace. According to the December 2019 menu at Les Deux Magots on the Place Saint-Germain-des-Prés, a coffee will cost you €4.90 at a table inside or on the stoep. It comes from a filter coffee pot and is the same price as a Grand Cru Arabica Espresso, which is as black as coal. If you're daft enough to want to add milk, they ask an additional €5.00. For the record, a latte costs €6.30 and a cappuccino €7.50. Quand même!

Thankfully, things look a little better here in the countryside. The locals moan about the outrageous price of €2.50. But what could be better than sitting under a bright-red umbrella on a sunny summer's day, watching the passing parade?

What has also changed is that you'll most likely hear Afrikaans while you're nonchalantly sipping your coffee. As I mentioned earlier, over 25 South African families have come to live in Boussac since we first set foot in France. The newest acquisition – by friends of ours – is the castle just outside the village with the drawbridge over the moat.

An atmosphere of hearty bonhomie prevails over the village in the summer, especially on Thursdays, which is market day. Everything that breathes heads for the stoeps of the two cafés or the Turkish shawarma restaurant. Lattes and cappuccinos are polished off at a fraction of Parisian prices.

Some of the more inventive South Africans have started a seasonal art gallery, a guesthouse and a shop in the small community. Another two shops and a *glacier* (ice-cream maker) will open soon, in the summer.

In the meantime, we've bought a beautiful old 17th-century building on Boussac's church square, from where I run my gallery and a little shop called Le Store. The building is a three-storey house with a lovely view of the Catholic church.

A group has even been founded to foster integration between newcomers and the French. It calls itself Amitiés Internationales du Pays de Boussac. Newcomers make friends and learn to speak French, the biggest hurdle for a new Boussacain. It took us four or five years to be able to hold a conversation without mistakes, but for us it was a question of sinking or swimming. There are also walking and cycling sessions every Thursday, for those who want to keep fit while continuing their conversations.

Another positive development is that many of the young people who moved to the big cities in previous years are coming back to the countryside. They're disillusioned by the high cost of living in the city, and come in search of the peace and simplicity that only the countryside can offer.

The village's Hotel Central has recently been bought by a young chef and his lovely wife, and transformed into a modern, elegant space. Their lunches are superb; you'll need to book far in advance to get a table on a Thursday. The chef's modern version of the classic confit de canard is legendary, and explains the restaurant's success.

All of this gives the once-quiet countryside an energetic kick-start. It's wonderful to sit on Boussac's town square, getting some perspective on life to the strains of French, English, Dutch and Afrikaans. After your second cup of coffee, the church tower announces lunchtime with 12 weighty chimes.

The energy on the square shifts. The owners of the stalls pack up their wares, like clockwork. The cheesemaker wraps damp cloths around his top sellers, the organic farmer packs bags of sweet tomatoes into a cardboard box, and the old lady with the bunches of wildflowers gives one to our assistant, who has just closed our shop.

It's been a good morning, but for now the work is put aside. À bientôt, until we meet again.

I must run. Hardy says the food is on the table.